" 'Cuckooing' is a complex problem that presents significant challenges for those involved in policy and practice. In this book, Spicer, an expert on drugs policing and county lines drug supply, draws on original empirical research to provide an innovative analysis of cuckooing through the public health-oriented conceptual framework of the 'risk environment'. It is an important inter-disciplinary contribution that should be read by everyone who wants to deepen their understanding of cuckooing and how to reduce drug market-related harms."

–**Dr Matthew Bacon,** *The University of Sheffield*

Cuckoo Land

Drawing on rich qualitative data, this book presents a novel way of understanding the drug market-related harm of 'cuckooing', providing a theoretically informed account of this increasingly high-profile area.

Applying the framework of the 'risk environment', the book examines why people become cuckooed, how it is responded to and how this exploitative practice is socially produced. In doing so, a diverse range of environments and features relevant to cuckooing are analysed, including the role of housing, political economy, drug policy, policing and social exclusion. By interrogating how these constrain and enable the actions of people who are affected, the book develops a critical analysis that recognises the complexity of cuckooing while eschewing superficial explanations of why it occurs. Resisting simplistic solutions, it also considers what an enabling environment capable of reducing the harms of this exploitative practice might look like.

Cuckoo Land will be of interest to academic researchers in the fields of criminology, victimology, social work and drugs. It will also be essential reading for policymakers and practitioners working on the issue of cuckooing.

Jack Spicer is a lecturer in criminology at the University of Bath.

Drugs, Crime and Society
Series Editors: Jack Spicer and Mark Monaghan

This new series will be a natural home for research on the topic of drugs and crime, bringing together original, innovative and topical books that, broadly conceived, address the role and impact of drugs and drugs policy on crime, criminality the criminal justice system and its agents. Aiming to showcase cutting edge theory and research in the area, it will serve as a focal point around which the field can continue to develop and flourish. Welcoming both research monographs and edited volumes, the series will serve as an outlet for exceptional early career researchers, established scholars and productive collaborations between those working in the field, across the globe.

The Cannabis Social Club
Mafalda Pardal

Cannabis Criminology
Johannes Wheeldon and Jon Heidt

Disneyization of Drug Use
Understanding Atypical Intoxication in Party Zones
Tim Turner

Mexico's Drug-Related Violence
Omar Camarillo

Towards Drug Policy Justice
Harm Reduction, Human Rights and Changing Drug Policy Contexts
Edited by Damon Barrett and Rick Lines

Cuckoo Land
The Cuckooing Risk Environment
Jack Spicer

For more information about this series, please visit: www.routledge.com/Drugs-Crime-and-Society/book-series/DCS

Cuckoo Land

The Cuckooing Risk Environment

Jack Spicer

LONDON AND NEW YORK

First published 2025
by Routledge
4 Park Square, Milton Park, Abingdon, Oxon OX14 4RN

and by Routledge
605 Third Avenue, New York, NY 10158

Routledge is an imprint of the Taylor & Francis Group, an informa business

British Library Cataloguing-in-Publication Data
A catalogue record for this book is available from the British Library

Library of Congress Cataloging-in-Publication Data
Names: Spicer, Jack (Lecturer in criminology), author.
Title: Cuckoo land : the cuckooing risk environment / Jack Spicer.
Description: Abingdon, Oxon ; New York, NY : Routledge, 2024. | Series: Drugs, crime and society | Includes bibliographical references and index.
Identifiers: LCCN 2024016900 (print) | LCCN 2024016901 (ebook) | ISBN 9781032705460 (hardback) | ISBN 9781032705491 (paperback) | ISBN 9781032705569 (ebook)
Subjects: LCSH: Drug traffic—Social aspects. | Swindlers and swindling. | Risk.
Classification: LCC HV5801 .S6468 2024 (print) | LCC HV5801 (ebook) | DDC 364.1/3365—dc23/eng/20240516
LC record available at https://lccn.loc.gov/2024016900
LC ebook record available at https://lccn.loc.gov/2024016901

ISBN: 978-1-032-70546-0 (hbk)
ISBN: 978-1-032-70549-1 (pbk)
ISBN: 978-1-032-70556-9 (ebk)

DOI: 10.4324/9781032705569

Typeset in Times New Roman
by Apex CoVantage, LLC

For Mum

Contents

Acknowledgements

I started writing this book shortly after joining the University of Bath in August 2022. Thanks to everyone who has welcomed me and offered support, guidance and encouragement with this project. A special mention is due to Rachel Willis for organising the departmental writing retreats where I was able to put pen to paper on much of this book's content.

Thanks to Ian Walmsley for continuing to provide enthusiasm for my ideas and a critical eye when I attempt to put them down in writing. This book has benefited greatly from our discussions. Long may they continue.

I'm indebted to all those who have facilitated or participated in my research. In a world where people are increasingly rushed and pressurised, it is a privilege to have people share their valuable time, stories and insights. Without it, books like this would not be possible.

I'm very grateful to my family and friends for consistently reminding me how important the world outside of academia is.

Thanks to Giulia for filling that world with her love.

1 Introduction

Over the past decade, a particular form of drug market-related harm, referred to as 'cuckooing', has become increasingly identified in the UK. Put simply, 'cuckooing' is the term used to describe situations where people have their homes taken over by others against their will, with its etymology linked to how wild cuckoos invade the nests of other birds. Understood as a highly exploitative practice, those who have their homes taken over are typically considered to be 'vulnerable' in some way (Moyle 2019). Having attracted considerable attention, it is now widely viewed as a pernicious problem that those involved in policy and practice are increasingly aware of and seeking to respond to.

Although not exclusive to drug market contexts (Macdonald et al. 2022), the construction of the cuckooing problem and the dominant understandings surrounding it have been based on a 'common scenario' (NCA 2018) where those involved in drug dealing, often through the so-called 'County Lines' supply methodology, take over the home of someone who uses drugs. Accordingly, HMICFRS (2023) define cuckooing as follows:

> A tactic where a drug dealer (or network) takes over a vulnerable person's home to prepare, store or deal drugs. It is commonly associated with exploitation and violence.

The involvement of drug-related actors, their motivations for engaging in cuckooing and its close association with the County Lines phenomenon have led to it being established as a drug market-related harm. Accordingly, a range of responses and activities have been initiated, led chiefly by the police and supported by other organisations including social work, housing and drug services (Spicer 2021a). As is common with drug law enforcement, this has regularly been complemented by 'symbolic' promotion of this work (Coomber et al. 2023).

Incidences of what are now widely referred to as 'cuckooing' have inevitably been occurring long before the term became widely used and recognised. This problem is therefore not completely 'new' nor without precedent. What

DOI: 10.4324/9781032705569-1

can be considered 'new', however, is how it has entered policy and practitioner lexicon and become established as a high-profile drug market-related harm necessitating significant responses. With attention rippling out into wider societal concern and awareness (CSJ 2021), the subject of cuckooing is ripe for research. Building on the small body of existing literature published by myself and others, this book attempts to make a novel and critical contribution to this important area. Through an empirically grounded, theoretically informed analysis, it sets out to achieve this by proposing the notion of the cuckooing 'risk environment'. Discussed in more detail later in this chapter, the public health-orientated conceptual framework of the 'risk environment' (Rhodes 2002) is useful for analysing this problem, as it allows for a novel way of both understanding it and thinking about how it can be ameliorated. Building on its legacy of addressing other harms associated with drug use, applying the risk environment framework to the criminological concern of cuckooing provides an original lens to view this drug market-related problem through and to analyse how it is structurally 'produced'.

As a criminologist interested in the murky world of illicit drug markets and the responses to them, cuckooing is an intriguing area to study. Since becoming exposed to the existence of this exploitative practice when embarking on my doctoral studies, I have spent considerable time listening, talking and thinking about it ever since. Whether it be presenting research to practitioners, speaking with academic colleagues or in the process of writing this book, what has become clear is that ameliorating this problem and reducing its harms are not an easy task. Straightforward accounts of why and how cuckooing occurs that fit comfortably into neat analytical explanations are hard to come by and rarely convincing when proposed, as demonstrated by recent interventions by several politicians (The Guardian 2023). In fact, a core aim of this book is an attempt to acknowledge and wrestle with all the complexities surrounding cuckooing – as uncomfortable and frustrating as it may be – rather than falling into the trap of smoothing them over to allow for simple explanations of why people become cuckooed and how we should respond. As appealing as these can be, this is too important an area for superficial explanations. Too many people continue to suffer terrible ordeals in the place where they should feel safe and secure. Considerable resources, time and energy also continue to be spent responding to this problem. Following the 'realist' criminological tradition (Matthews 2014; Stevens 2020), this book therefore attempts to take cuckooing 'seriously' by acknowledging its complex reality and recognising it as a very real harm. Doing so opens the door to developing a deep, rigorous analysis.

The remainder of this chapter sets out three core areas that represent the foundation for the rest of the book. First, regarding the book's subject matter, a discussion on the topic of cuckooing is provided. Second, at the level of theory, the conceptual framework of the risk environment is outlined, alongside a justification for why a risk environment-informed analysis of this criminological area is worthwhile. Finally, a methodological note on the qualitative data reported in this book and its analysis is provided.

Cuckooing

It is worth noting that, at the time of writing, the act of 'cuckooing' is not itself a criminal offence. While recent calls have been made to close this perceived criminal justice 'gap' (CSJ 2021), a person cannot currently be convicted of having 'cuckooed' someone else. However, there are criminal offences that inevitably take place either as part of or alongside these scenarios. Because of the typical actors involved, drug offences are regularly a central occurrence in the homes that are taken over, with these domestic spaces used to store and supply drugs (Coomber and Moyle 2018). Those affected may also experience threats, coercion and violence (Robinson et al. 2019). Recognising this, it is arguably appropriate to conceptualise cuckooing as a drug market-related 'harm'. As demonstrated by the terminology used so far in this chapter, this is the position taken in this book. In one sense, conceptualising cuckooing as a 'harm' is a pragmatic decision based on its (lack of) legal status. On a more theoretical level, doing so usefully opens the door for it to be analysed through the drug policy lens of 'harm reduction'.

The legal ambiguity surrounding cuckooing is demonstrative of its wider complexity. One central aspect of this, comprising a core concern of this book, revolves around what it means to be a 'victim' of cuckooing and to be recognised as such by others. Often being users of heroin and crack cocaine, alongside having criminal records and hostile relationships with societal institutions, those affected regularly fall short of presenting as 'ideal victims' (Christie 1986). Framed through the policy discourse of 'vulnerability', the extent to which their actions may have led to drug dealers having a presence in their home, alongside a broader capacity for agency, is also a common point of contention (Moyle 2019; Spicer 2021a). This tension is visible in Crown Prosecution Service guidance (CPS 2022) stating:

> Victimhood of cuckooed property occupants is variable and a full investigation of the circumstances of that occupier should be carried out by police and partner agencies.

The extent to which certain indoor drug-using environments, containing people who use and sell drugs, constitute 'cuckooing' or whether they are interpreted more in line with notions of 'crack houses' (Briggs 2010) is therefore morally contentious. Overlapping with this, it also raises practical challenges for people working in this area of how to respond appropriately and effectively to cuckooing (MacDonald et al. 2022; Spicer 2021b).

The complexity surrounding cuckooing formed the basis for an article I published with Leah Moyle and Ross Coomber, where we attempted to provide the first thorough academic interrogation of the subject (see Spicer et al. 2020). Considering cuckooing as an umbrella term that encompasses a variety of situations, we proposed a four-fold typology that is worth briefly sketching out.

Following its etymology, cuckooing cases described as 'parasitic nest invading' involve the most 'clear-cut' forms of exploitative home takeovers. Access to the homes of those affected is achieved via deception or force, with violence used by dealers to maintain their use of this space. In comparison, cases described as 'quasi-cuckooing' involve greater agency of those affected. Initial access to their homes in these cases is acquired via people being offered money, drugs or sometimes just company. The extent to which they are aware of their 'guests' intentions can vary in these cases. However, while initial complicity of some form is observable, this soon fades once their home becomes taken over and they experience threats, intimidation and violence when attempting to terminate the situation. The third type of cuckooing cases we identified has a gendered aspect and is described as 'coupling'. These revolve around some form of sexual relationship, usually between a male dealer and a female resident, with this used as a way of both obtaining and maintaining access to a home that is taken over. Such cases add further complexity to understandings of cuckooing as an exploitative practice, not least because cases within this type can vary from those that appear to involve cynical 'faux-romantic relationship' to those that involve disturbing sexual violence.

The final type of cuckooing within Spicer et al. (2020) is what we refer to as 'local' cuckooing and involves cases that explicitly sit outside of 'County Lines' drug supply. This retail-level heroin and crack supply model has generated significant attention over recent years in the UK and involves networks from major conurbations servicing drug markets in provincial areas. Much has been written about County Lines and its various features (see e.g. Densley et al. 2023; Harding 2020; Marshall 2023; Robinson et al. 2019). Most important in the context of this book is how cuckooing is routinely embedded within it. In short, dealers spending time in satellite locations need somewhere to base themselves, as well as store money and drugs. This is typically achieved by taking over the home of a local resident, whom they often become exposed to via the illicit drug market. Because of the close connection between cuckooing and County Lines, the previous three types are predicated on them involving 'out-of-town' dealers taking over the homes of local residents. The final type of 'local' cuckooing, however, highlights the capacity for scenarios where people take over the homes of other people in the area where they live. While these cases are still appropriately understood as 'cuckooing', their occurrence is not because dealers are 'foreign' to the area and are without a base. Instead, by not wanting to bring their business 'home' it is seemingly adopted as a 'defensive strategy' (see Buerger 1992) to develop barriers to police attention.

This typology proposed in Spicer et al. (2020) is not necessarily exhaustive. As highlighted in the article's title, cuckooing should be understood as an 'evolving' practice that, just like other drug market-related harms, has the capacity to change and develop over time. However, given the current state of knowledge about cuckooing, the typology provides a way of recognising how and why it can occur, as well as the differences that exist between cases. Others have seemingly found it a useful way of thinking about and identifying the cases they have come across in their research projects (e.g. Holligan et al. 2020). Accordingly, the types are regularly drawn on to make sense of the cases discussed in this book.

This typology was also not intended to be the 'final word' on the subject. Rather, it was hoped that future studies could situate themselves within it and build on its insights. Harding's (2020) discussion of the approaches of County Lines dealers when cuckooing people is a good example of this, with factors such as location, urgency and access identified as key features that are navigated when successfully achieving and maintaining access to people's homes. Importantly, he also highlights the complex relationship between 'cuckooing' drug dealers and the affected residents, with the varied and nuanced strategies adopted by this population when faced with having others use their home ranging from passive compliance to more agentic forms of resistance to regain some control. The consideration of agency among the 'vulnerable' people affected by cuckooing is also recognised by Moyle (2019), as well as being situated in Densley et al.'s (2023) robust challenge of the wider discourses surrounding County Lines that have emerged over recent years. Away from County Lines, Macdonald et al. (2022) have importantly stressed the capacity for cuckooing to manifest as a form of 'mate crime' against disabled people, opening a further avenue to explore in future cuckooing studies that are not necessarily orientated only around drug markets.

All these insights provide a useful foundation to build on. However, analysing the practice of cuckooing itself provides only a partial story. Understandings of this area must also be grounded in an interrogation of the responses to it. As noted at the start of this chapter, the police have been central in constructing and defining the 'problem' of cuckooing, as well as the main leaders of the responses enacted against it (Coliandris 2015). My ethnographic fieldwork has shone a light on the reality of some of the practices pursued by police officers, including how tactics such as 'welfare checks' are used and experienced within this context (Spicer 2021a, see also Harding 2020). Perhaps more critically, I have also argued that an 'amplification spiral' has occurred around the policing of this area (Spicer 2021b). Starting from its construction as a 'problem' through to its establishment as an area of policing priority, the various stages of the police response to cuckooing have not eliminated this drug market-related harm, despite 'symbolic' claims of apparent success (Coomber et al. 2023). Instead, both in the material reality of the practice and among the perceptions of police officers, other agencies and wider communities, the problem of cuckooing appears to have become amplified through a symbiotic relationship with the responses to it. The nature of this relationship, combined with the wider challenges of recognising 'victimhood' and 'vulnerability' among those affected, further stresses the complexity of cuckooing. Analysis of this area must therefore consider both the immediate acts of cuckooing and the reactions to it.

Drug-related harms and risk environments

Drug-related harms are diverse, evolving and complex. They intersect with, reproduce and can mask structural issues including economic inequality, racial injustice, gendered discrimination and stigmatisation (Bourgois 2003). Experiencing these harms can be a chronic feature of people's lives, often situated among a range of other social problems and a wider backdrop of marginality (Collins et al. 2019). This poses significant challenges to the attempts to reduce them. Accordingly, attempts at reducing drug-related harms are far from universally successful, with their impact varying widely. As the chequered history of drug policy demonstrates, some interventions can be life-saving and emancipatory. Others, however, can be ineffective or even generate harms themselves (Ritter 2022).

As a result of their diversity, drug-related harms are sometimes grouped into a range of different categories by those working in the field. The negative health outcomes experienced by people who use drugs are a common example (Degenhardt et al. 2023). The various (un)intended consequences of drug policy are another (Cooper 2015). Yet the boundaries between these categories are often blurred and far from mutually exclusive. In particular, the various harms associated with the functioning of illicit drug markets, which have typically been the focus of criminological analysis, arguably share many characteristics with other drug-related harms, which have traditionally been the disciplinary focus of public health. There is arguably an advantage in bringing these perspectives together and avoiding the compartmentalisation of such harms. For example, in addition to affecting similar populations, both drug market-related harms (e.g. supply-related violence) and harms associated with drug use (e.g. transmission of blood-borne viruses) can generate considerable attention and heightened social anxiety while being vulnerable to misunderstanding and distortion through how they are portrayed. In addition, it is common to witness stakeholders competing to define the underlying problem perceived to be causing these harms and to take ownership of leading the response (Reinarman and Levine 1989; Stevens 2024). Regardless of who ultimately wins this competition for ownership, if the inherent complexity of these harms is not adequately recognised, and simplistic, ill-informed ideas are pursued, the chances of ameliorating them are reduced (Ritter 2022).

To critically analyse drug-related harms, whether they are associated with use, markets, or both, appropriate concepts and theories are required (Stevens

2020). Since being proposed two decades ago (Rhodes 2002), the 'risk environment' has become one of the most influential analytic frameworks in the drug policy field. Described as a "*social science for harm reduction*" (Rhodes 2009, p. 198), it has informed a significant body of research unified by the goal of identifying and addressing the social and structural drivers of drug-related harm. Its original formulation emerged from a critique of public health interventions that overly focused on individualistic modes of behaviour change (Rhodes et al. 2003). These interventions, such as those aimed at reducing HIV infection, were argued to conceptualise targeted populations as rational decision-makers. People who inject drugs, for example, were expected to incorporate the information imparted to them into their decisions and become empowered to take responsibility for their health (Walmsley 2012). They were expected to consider relevant risks such as contracting a blood-borne virus and subsequently act in ways that minimised them. Those who did not follow this advice or engage with harm reduction interventions as intended were considered irrational, dysfunctional and potentially blameworthy for the harms they experienced (see Kelly 2005; Moore and Fraser 2006). Proposing an alternative, ecologically based approach, the risk environment framework instead stresses the importance of the dynamic relationship between people who use drugs and the environments where they spend their time, make decisions and live their lives.

Broadly defined as "*the space – whether social or physical – in which a variety of factors interact to increase the chances of drug related harm*" (Rhodes 2002, p. 91), the various factors exogenous to the individual are moved to the foreground through the notion of the 'risk environment'. These factors are suggested as not only inescapable but fundamental to shaping the nature, context and experience of drug harms. As a conceptual framework, the risk environment draws attention to the socially constructed nature of 'harm' and the subjectivity of 'risk' (Moore and Dietz 2005). It recognises that harm reduction interventions do not take place in sterile, laboratory-like conditions but are inescapably social in nature (Rhodes et al. 2003). It stresses the limitations of context-free decision-making theories, where risk avoidance is often synonymous with rationality, to ones where risk, its perception and how this is acted upon are viewed as inherently risk- and context-dependent (Collins et al. 2019). As Rhodes (2009, p. 194) states, a risk environment approach shifts the focus from the unit of the individual and individual-level change to "*the social situations and structures in which they find themselves*".

The totality of a 'risk environment', with its various features capable of both producing and reducing drug-related harm, comprises two key dimensions. These are the *types* of environments and *levels* of environmental influence (Rhodes 2002). Regarding the former, four 'ideal' environment types are identified: 'physical', 'social', 'economic', and 'policy'. Linking to the latter, these are recognised as intersecting and interacting at the micro and macro levels. Examples of micro-level environments include the immediate physical settings where drugs are used and the cultural norms that exist within social groups. Examples at the macro level include legal contexts that control drug use and structural inequalities that influence the resources people have available to them.

The emphasis on the interaction between these types of environments and the level at which they operate demonstrates a core theoretical influence in the form of 'structuration' (Giddens 1984). While the conception of the risk environment stresses the role and influence of social structures, it simultaneously commits to "*understanding how risk environments are experienced and embodied as part of everyday practices*" (Rhodes 2009, p. 194). As a process, structuration provides a useful theoretical bridge, conceptualising individual agents and social structures as adaptive and reflective of each other through what Giddens (1984) famously refers to as the 'duality of structure'. In short, rather than being held as separate, structure and agency are considered two sides of the same coin. Agency is preceded by often unacknowledged structures, which provide necessary conditions for action to take place. Yet structures are also the outcomes of actions, with often unacknowledged outcomes serving to transform or reproduce them (Stones 2005). Aligning with the notion of structure being simultaneously constraining and enabling, through the risk environment framework, a practical aim is to consider what an 'enabling environment' could look like for reducing drug-related harms, including what structural and situational interventions could be introduced to enable harm reduction (Moore and Dietz 2005). These changes can be 'polythetic', whereby barriers and environmental obstacles to harm reduction are systematically removed, or they can be 'monothetic', whereby initiatives or interventions that maximise harm reduction effects are introduced (Rhodes 2002).

The risk environment framework's influence on the drugs field has been significant, with an abundance of studies deploying it. Two are worth briefly detailing here for illustrative purposes. Rhodes et al.'s (2005) review of the risk environment for HIV infection among injecting drug users serves as a classic example. Based on a sweeping review of relevant evidence, they analyse a range of relevant factors that span across different types of the environment and exert influence at the micro and macro levels. These include the movement of populations, transitions within the political and economic spheres, the role of stigma, political and economic inequalities, and the immediate environments where drugs are injected. All of these are argued to be central to producing HIV risk and must therefore be placed centrally in attempts to understand and reduce it.

A slightly different example of a risk environment study is visible in the work of McNeil et al. (2014), who consider hospitals as specific risk environments for people who inject drugs. Focusing on this specific physical and social setting, they detail the intersecting structural factors that lead to this population being disproportionately discharged against medical advice, resulting in elevated risks of readmission, longer stays and morbidity. These range from inadequate pain management provision to stigmatisation. Of course, countless other risk environment-informed analyses could be cited here. But for the purposes of this book, the key point is the capacity of this framework to think about and address drug-related harms in a way that is theoretically sophisticated, critically informed and practically orientated. This has great potential when it comes to the subject of cuckooing.

Towards a cuckooing risk environment

Following these insights a three-fold justification can be made for taking a risk environment approach to the area of cuckooing. First, as detailed in Spicer (2021a), many of the current responses to cuckooing fall into the trap of overly focusing on individual behaviour change, with those affected or considered 'at risk' encouraged to take actions that keep themselves 'safe' because they are 'vulnerable'. Examples that I have observed from police officers and other professionals include asking people not to allow anyone to enter their home, telling them to avoid socialising with people outside of it and admonishing them because they "didn't ask for help" when becoming affected. Through the lens of the risk environment framework, this ignores the wider context and can lead to those affected being misunderstood or even blamed for the harms they experience.

Second, as argued in relation to the notion of an 'amplification spiral' (Spicer 2021b), while success is achieved by the police and others at preventing some people becoming cuckooed or removing those affected from harmful situations, a frequent outcome is that the perpetrators simply move elsewhere. Not only can this render the responses to cuckooing somewhat ineffective, but at worse it can risk spreading the problem to greater numbers of people and communities, creating more victims who might experience even worse exploitation. In this sense, considering the structural and social drivers of cuckooing represents a potentially more effective way of both understanding the problem and helping to point towards how the ground-level interventions may become more effective.

This leads to the third and final justification, which concerns the potential direction that responses to cuckooing may be heading. A report by the influential think tank, *The Centre for Social Justice*, for example, has promoted ratcheting up the legal consequences for those involved (see CSJ 2021). Combined with other similar proposals, this suggests that a 'law and order' oriented, punitive approach may well be pursued by those in the policy arena in the near future. A risk environment analysis challenges this and provides an alternative perspective.

It is also worth considering the broader theoretical implications of applying the risk environment framework to the area of cuckooing for the discipline of criminology. As previously identified, risk environment analyses have traditionally focused on drug-related harms that are typically the preserve of the public health field, with the health harms experienced by people who use drugs a classic example. The framework has been directly applied far less to harms associated with the functioning of illicit drug markets and the activities of the actors involved. Some studies have pointed towards the potential fruitfulness of doing so. Fitzgerald's (2009) analysis of two 'dealing houses', for example, demonstrates how supply actors simultaneously shape and are shaped by their risk environment. Through this lens, he sheds light on important criminological concerns, including the complexity of drug market violence, the social nature of economic relations between drug market actors (see also Dwyer and Moore 2010), and the role of community resilience. Similarly, albeit in a different setting, Moyle and Coomber's (2019) consideration of university student involvement in drug supply demonstrates a valuable way of appreciating relevant features of universities and how they interact with the drug market. By deploying the risk environment framework, they provide a detailed, contextual account of the range of structural factors that can lead to young people transitioning into drug supply activity within this particular physical and social environment.

In keeping with its 'rendezvous' tradition there appears significant capacity for criminological work to continue to build on this and take inspiration from the wider drugs field to inform its analysis of drug market activity. At a time of increased championing of a 'public health' approach to policing and engagement with 'vulnerable' people, there are clear potential benefits of drawing on established public health frameworks. Doing so adds greater depth to interdisciplinary ambitions while narrowing the distance between these and the theoretical approaches traditionally used within criminology. In addition to making an important contribution to the specific area of cuckooing, by developing a risk environment analysis for this drug market context, this book therefore also attempts to further this theoretical endeavour.

A methodological note

The analysis presented in the subsequent chapters of this book is primarily based on a range of in-depth interviews I conducted during 2021 and 2022 with practitioners who had significant exposure to cases of cuckooing and experience of engaging with people affected by it. Twenty-six interviews were conducted in total, with the standard ethical conventions of informed consent, anonymity and confidentiality adhered to. Broken down by role, the interviewees comprised seven police officers (two sergeants and five constables); six housing officers; four drug service workers; four outreach workers; two drug service managers; two social workers; and one criminal justice worker. The cases of cuckooing they discussed were based on their experiences working across a medium-sized city, a smaller city and three medium-sized towns in the South of England, all of which I have kept anonymous.

Supplementing these interviews, I was also able to shadow several of the police officers, housing officers and outreach workers during their working days and accompany them on visits to people they worked with. To supplement this phase of data collection, at times in the following chapters, I also draw on previous experiences during my ethnographic doctoral fieldwork (see Spicer 2021a), as well as data from existing published literature. This is done partly to flesh out pertinent points raised in the analysis regarding identified features of the cuckooing risk environment. By drawing on quotes from those who have been directly cuckooed, it is also a way of partially remedying the lack of those directly affected by cuckooing within the interview data collected for this project.

While left suitably open to allow for rich detail, the structure and content of the interviews were guided by the risk environment framework. Many of the questions were designed to elicit what the 'cuckooing risk environment' consisted of. In line with how Giddens (1984) conceived it, structuration theory was also treated as a 'sensitising device'. Before the interviews began, the people I spoke to were given a brief explanation about the risk environment as part of a general overview about the study and why I wanted to speak with them. This was done for the sake of transparency, while helping to set the context for the type of insights I was looking to generate. The risk environment framework also served as a tool to structure the analysis of the interview data. Following Layder's (1998) 'adaptive theory' approach, I used the types and levels of environment set out in Rhodes (2002) as initial broad organising codes. I then went on to develop these through an iterative process of inductively driven analysis of the data, combined with drawing on a diverse range of sociological, criminological and public health concepts.

Following this process of analysis, five core features of the risk environment were constructed. These serve to structure the book and are set out in turn in the following chapters. Chapter 2 focuses on the economic environment, analysing the various features of this environment type that makes people structurally vulnerable to cuckooing and the role of their agency within these constraints. Chapter 3 places its attention on the physical environment, considering its various features relevant to cuckooing at the micro-level of people's homes, the meso-level of people's neighbourhoods and the macro-level of geographic locations. Chapter 4 focuses specifically on the role of drug policy as a core feature of the policy environment, using the three areas of market prohibition, criminalisation of possession and drug treatment to analyse the role this area of policy plays in the lives of those affected by cuckooing. Focusing on the responses to this harm, Chapter 5 scrutinises the policing of the cuckooing risk environment, considering how the police (re)produce certain features, how their actions are viewed by other agencies and the constraints officers face in their work. Chapter 6 provides the final empirically based analysis by looking at the social environment. Making links between macro- and micro-level features, the analysis considers how features such as social exclusion, (sub)cultural norms and feelings of shame can serve to produce vulnerability to cuckooing. The book's final chapter concludes by setting out core aspects of the cuckooing risk environment, what an 'enabling environment' for reducing cuckooing might look like and the implications of this analysis for future policy, practice and research agendas.

References

Bourgois, P. (2003) *In Search of Respect* (2nd edition). Cambridge: Cambridge University Press.

Briggs, D. (2010) Crack houses in the UK: Some observations on their operations. *Drugs and Alcohol Today*. 10 (4), pp. 33–42.

Buerger, M. (1992) Defensive strategies of the street-level drug trade. *Journal of Crime and Justice*. 15 (2), pp. 31–51.

Christie, N. (1986) The ideal victim. In: E. Fattah (ed). *From Crime Policy to Victim Policy*. London: Palgrave Macmillan, pp. 17–30.

Coliandris, G. (2015) County lines and wicked problems: Exploring the need for improved policing approaches to vulnerability and early intervention. *Australasian Policing: A Journal of Professional Practice and Research*. 7 (2), pp. 25–36.

Collins, A. B., Boyd, J., Cooper, H. L. and McNeil, R. (2019) The intersectional risk environment of people who use drugs. *Social Science & Medicine*. DOI: https://doi.org/10.1016/j.socscimed.2019.112384

Coomber, R., Bacon, M., Spicer, J. and Moyle, L. (2023) Symbolic drugs policing: Conceptual development and harm reduction opportunities. In: M. Bacon and J. Spicer (eds). *Drug Law Enforcement, Policing and Harm Reduction: Ending the Stalemate*. London: Routledge, pp. 87–110.

Coomber, R. and Moyle, L. (2018) The changing shape of street-level heroin and crack supply in England: Commuting, holidaying and cuckooing drug dealers across 'county lines'. *British Journal of Criminology*. 58 (6), pp. 1323–1342.

Cooper, H. L. (2015) War on drugs policing and police brutality. *Substance Use & Misuse*. 50 (8–9), pp. 1188–1194.

CPS (2022) *County Lines Offending*. Available from: www.cps.gov.uk/legal-guidance/county-lines-offending [Accessed 2 November 2023]

CSJ (2021) *Cuckooing: The Case for Strengthening the Law against Slavery in the Home*. London: Centre for Social Justice.

Degenhardt, L., Webb, P., Colledge-Frisby, S., Ireland, J., Wheeler, A., Ottaviano, S., Willing, A., Kairouz, A., Cunningham, E. B., Hajarizadeh, B. and Leung, J. (2023) Epidemiology of injecting drug use, prevalence of injecting-related harm, and exposure to behavioural and environmental risks among people who inject drugs: A systematic review. *The Lancet Global Health*. DOI: https://doi.org/10.1016/S2214-109X(23)00057-8

Densley, J., McLean, R. and Brick, C. (2023) *Contesting County Lines: Case Studies in Drug Crime and Deviant Entrepreneurship*. Bristol: Policy Press.

Dwyer, R. and Moore, D. (2010) Understanding illicit drug markets in Australia: Notes towards a critical reconceptualization. *The British Journal of Criminology*. 50 (1), pp. 82–101.

Fitzgerald, J. L. (2009) Mapping the experience of drug dealing risk environments: An ethnographic case study. *International Journal of Drug Policy*. 20 (3), pp. 261–269.

Giddens, A. (1984) *The Constitution of Society*. Cambridge: Polity.

The Guardian (2023) *Jess Phillips and Iain Duncan Smith Lead Calls to Criminalise 'Cuckooing'*. Available from: www.theguardian.com/uk-news/2023/feb/26/jess-phillips-and-iain-duncan-smith-lead-calls-to-criminalise-cuckooing [Accessed 2 November 2023]

Harding, S. (2020) *County Lines: Exploitation and Drug Dealing among Urban Street Gangs*. Bristol: Policy Press.

HMICFRS (2023) *Cuckooing*. Available from: https://hmicfrs.justiceinspectorates.gov.uk/glossary/cuckooing/ [Accessed 2 November 2023]

Holligan, C., McLean, R. and McHugh, R. (2020) Exploring County lines: Criminal drug distribution practices in Scotland. *Youth Justice*. 20(1–2), pp. 50–63.

Kelly, B. C. (2005) Conceptions of risk in the lives of club drug-using youth. *Substance Use & Misuse*. 40 (9–10), pp. 1443–1459.

Layder, D. (1998) *Sociological Practice: Linking Theory and Social Research*. London: Sage.

Macdonald, S. J., Donovan, C., Clayton, J. and Husband, M. (2022) Becoming cuckooed: Conceptualising the relationship between disability, home takeovers and criminal exploitation. *Disability & Society*. DOI: https://doi.org/10.1080/09687599.2022.2071680

Marshall, H. (2023) Victim as a relative status. *Theoretical Criminology*. DOI: https://doi.org/10.1177/13624806231186393

Matthews, R. (2014) *Realist Criminology*. London: Springer.

McNeil, R., Small, W., Wood, E. and Kerr, T. (2014) Hospitals as a 'risk environment': An ethno-epidemiological study of voluntary and involuntary discharge from hospital against medical advice among people who inject drugs. *Social Science & Medicine*. 105, pp. 59–66.

Moore, D. and Dietze, P. (2005) Enabling environments and the reduction of drug-related harm: Re-framing Australian policy and practice. *Drug and Alcohol Review*. 24 (3), pp. 275–284.

Moore, D. and Fraser, S. (2006) Putting at risk what we know: Reflecting on the drug-using subject in harm reduction and its political implications. *Social Science & Medicine*. 62 (12), pp. 3035–3047.

Moyle, L. (2019) Situating vulnerability and exploitation in street-level drug markets: Cuckooing, commuting, and the 'county lines' drug supply model. *Journal of Drug Issues*. 49 (4), pp. 739–755.

Moyle, L. and Coomber, R. (2019) Student transitions into drug supply: Exploring the university as a 'risk environment'. *Journal of Youth Studies*. 22 (5), pp. 642–657.

NCA (2018) *County Lines Drug Supply, Vulnerability and Harm*. London: NCA.

Reinarman, C. and Levine, H. (1989) Crack in context: Politics and media in the making of a drug scare. *Contemporary Drug Problems*. 16 (4), pp. 535–577.

Rhodes, T. (2002) The 'risk environment': A framework for understanding and reducing drug-related harm. *International Journal of Drug Policy*. 13 (2), pp. 85–94.

Rhodes, T. (2009) Risk environments and drug harms: A social science for harm reduction approach. *International Journal of Drug Policy*. 20 (3), pp. 193–201.

Rhodes, T., Lilly, R., Fernández, C., Giorgino, E., Kemmesis, U. E., Ossebaard, H. C., Lalam, N., Faasen, I. and Spannow, K. E. (2003) Risk factors associated with drug use: The importance of 'risk environment'. *Drugs: Education, Prevention and Policy*. 10 (4), pp. 303–329.

Rhodes, T., Singer, M., Bourgois, P., Friedman, S. R. and Strathdee, S. A. (2005) The social structural production of HIV risk among injecting drug users. *Social Science & Medicine*. 61 (5), pp. 1026–1044.

Ritter, A. (2022) *Drug Policy*. London: Routledge.

Robinson, G., McLean, R. and Densley, J. (2019) Working county lines: Child criminal exploitation and illicit drug dealing in Glasgow and Merseyside. *International Journal of Offender Therapy and Comparative Criminology*. 63 (5), pp. 694–711.

Spicer, J. (2021a) *Policing County Lines*. London: Palgrave.

Spicer, J. (2021b) The policing of cuckooing in 'county lines' drug dealing: An ethnographic study of an amplification spiral. *The British Journal of Criminology*. 61 (5), pp. 1390–1406.

Spicer, J., Moyle, L. and Coomber, R. (2020) The variable and evolving nature of 'cuckooing' as a form of criminal exploitation in street level drug markets. *Trends in Organized Crime*. 23 (4), pp. 301–323.

Stevens, A. (2020) Critical realism and the 'ontological politics of drug policy'. *International Journal of Drug Policy*. DOI: https://doi.org/10.1016/j.drugpo.2020.102723

Stevens, A. (2024) *Drug Policy Constellations: The Role of Power and Morality in the Making of Drug Policy in the UK*. Bristol: Policy Press.

Stones, R. (2005) *Structuration Theory*. Basingstoke: Palgrave.

Walmsley, I. (2012) Governing the injecting drug user: Beyond needle fixation. *History of the Human Sciences*. 25 (4), pp. 90–107.

2 Cuckooing and the economic environment

This first empirically based chapter interrogates the role of the economic environment in producing cuckooing. Critical analyses of crime, harm and criminal justice grounded in the tradition of political economy have a productive history of scrutinising who breaks the law, who gets criminalised for it and why in relation to the dynamics of capitalist societies (e.g. Chambliss 1975). In the drugs field, risk environment studies have consistently identified economic factors at both the micro and macro levels as central to their analysis. More broadly, political economy has been used persuasively to explain the production of drug-related harms, their distribution across the social structure and how they can be reduced (Stevens 2011). Such issues, including deindustrialisation, unequal access to resources and labour market exclusion, therefore require suitable attention and must be adequately addressed if drug-related harms are to be meaningfully ameliorated (see Van Draanen et al. 2023, for a useful review).

This chapter takes inspiration from this to analyse the features of the economic environment pertinent to cuckooing and the role they can play in making people structurally vulnerable to being affected. The analytical approach taken naturally leans towards a structural orientation. However, in addition to highlighting relevant features of this type of environment and emphasising the significance of current economic arrangements in comprehending the occurrence of cuckooing, by drawing on several other theoretical tools, the chapter also considers the role of agency and human action within this structural context. Doing so avoids the tendency of political economic approaches to risk environment analyses of "*positioning individuals as largely passive in their complicity to structural determinants*" (Rhodes et al. 2012, p. 2023). Instead, by recognising affected people's capacity for agency within their economic constraints, the analysis attempts to remain attentive to the ultimately human context of cuckooing.

Political choices, the economy and cuckooing

Various observations in the existing literature on cuckooing point towards those affected being heavily concentrated among those experiencing socio-economic marginalisation (Harding 2020; Moyle 2019; Spicer et al. 2020).

DOI: 10.4324/9781032705569-2

Rather than allowing this to be an implicit and accepted feature of the cuckooing landscape, it is useful to bring it to the fore and consider more deeply the role that economic conditions can play in why many people become affected. Various people I interviewed were keen to stress that those people being affected by cuckooing were typically those exposed to the sharpest edges of the UK's economic system. Their daily lives were suggested to be a grinding ordeal of sometimes significant suffering, with harsh day-to-day existences resting on the back of years of economic marginalisation. During fieldwork, I visited many of these people, whose precarious existence regularly represented an accumulation of problems associated with deep and prolonged economic exclusion. This then often manifested in what was routinely labelled by practitioners as 'chaotic lifestyles'. In fact, while the context for visiting these people was about their risk of being cuckooed, it was not uncommon for interactions between them and the professionals I visited them with to be dominated by discussions about how to apply to certain welfare schemes or to make them aware of sources of support they were entitled to. Experiences of poverty therefore combined with a more general sense of material deprivation to form a consistent backdrop for most cuckooing cases.

The economic conditions that engulfed many of the people affected were therefore situated as the primary context for considering why people were vulnerable to cuckooing. A drug service manager discussed cuckooing in relation to the wider, intensifying experiences of deprivation and poverty faced by many of the people she worked with. As she described:

> I don't want to get too political about all this but the bar is so low at the moment. I mean, people are hungry, you know? They don't have their basic needs met. So when we're talking about vulnerability and cuckooing, well when you've got people in such poverty it's not hard to see how it happens.
>
> (Beth, drug service manager)

The role of economic marginalisation in producing vulnerability to becoming cuckooed appeared specifically relevant to 'quasi-cuckooing' cases (Spicer et al. 2020). As outlined in the opening chapter, these involve an initial form of willingness by an occupant for their home to be used by others based on perceived benefits such as offers of financial reimbursement before degenerating into an exploitative situation. Being in a financial position characterised by unemployment, insufficient welfare payments and increased living costs, combined with the cost of maintaining regular drug use, meant that for some, opportunities to generate income or otherwise alleviate their economic situation via facilitating access to their homes represented a rare opportunity in what were often desperate circumstances (see also Moyle 2019). As a drug service worker outlined, this 'choice' of initially facilitating access has to be understood within the context of the economic situation that many people who become embroiled in cuckooing find themselves, with it being fertile for people to become affected:

> It can be complicated, a bit muddy. I'd describe some of it like grooming behaviour. But you asked, "why do some of them let the dealers in in the first place?" Well, it's because they offer them something, don't they? And when you're skint and just constantly on that edge, a bit of money, even just a little bit, can be hard to turn down. It's easy to say it's stupid and wrong and all that. But until you're faced with that choice I don't think you can say you'd do anything differently.
>
> (Alex, drug service worker)

Situated within broader observations made in the drugs field, the apparent role of the economic circumstances of those typically affected by cuckooing is in some ways unsurprising. The links between certain types of drug use, drug markets, related harms and inequality have been well established. As Alex Stevens (2011) has demonstrated, the social distribution of drug harms is highly unequal. Put simply, despite data suggesting that illicit drug use in general is spread fairly consistently across society, those located towards the bottom of the social structure face a disproportionate amount and intensity of drug-related harm. This can relate to harms associated with drug use, with the cohort who makes up the majority of drug-related deaths in the UK a clear example (Stevens 2019). But overlapping with this, in the context of cuckooing, it is worth noting that these harms and their uneven distribution are also visible when it comes to the domain of drug supply. Drug markets are not all equal or necessarily similar (Coomber 2006). Instead, the most marginalised in society are typically exposed to some of the harshest, most volatile drug markets and associated conditions (Densley and Stevens 2015; Irwin-Rogers 2019). It is in these markets where harms such as cuckooing are often embedded.

These observations stress the importance of situating cuckooing within the wider economic arrangements of society. Macdonald et al. (2022) highlight the potential role of austerity policies in making people more vulnerable to cuckooing. As I have also argued elsewhere, the rise of cuckooing and the County Lines phenomenon more broadly has notably coincided with these political economic decisions (Spicer 2021a). Given the structural position of those typically affected and the apparent connection of this to experiences of socio-economic marginalisation, vulnerability to cuckooing must be understood within the context of inequality. This is especially the case given the tendency for inequality to be 'silenced' (Stevens 2011) or obscured through other means such as 'scapegoating' (Spicer 2021a). Both the economic arrangements and associated drug-related harms are predicated on political choices and moral positions about those who are (un)deserving (Stevens 2024; Wincup and Monaghan 2016). Rather than viewing these harms as inevitable, the important, emancipatory capacity of social policy to ameliorate them must be brought to the fore. Though sometimes overlooked by various stakeholders and influencers, the political economy of drug policy is essential to a serious interrogation of drug-related harm (Bourgois 2003a). Understanding the production of cuckooing as a drug market-related harm appears to be no different.

Contingent causation in the illicit economy

Having stressed the significance of political economy to the cuckooing risk environment context, it is worth turning to the complex micro-level relationship between cuckooing and economic conditions. Portraying the relationship between the economic environment and the reasons for why cuckooing occurs as being a simple causal link is unsatisfactory when attempting to develop a deeper and theoretically informed account that fits with the complex experiences of those affected. Acts of crime, deviance and transgression do not happen within a social, cultural and emotional vacuum. Suggesting that they do, often as a result of the methodological traps of 'abstract empiricism' or the deployment of 'grand theory', shuts down, or at least severely limits, an interrogation of the deeper mechanisms at play (Young 2011). Instead, aligning with the theoretical tenets of the risk environment framework, people actively engage with, shape and reproduce the environments around them (see Rhodes 2009). Acknowledging this in the context of cuckooing provides a vital further dimension when thinking about the role of the economic environment.

Demonstrating the complexity of this relationship, comparisons made by several of the interviewees between cuckooing and other potential means of attaining income highlighted the 'contingent causation' (Glass and McAtee 2006) between those affected by cuckooing and the structural restraints imposed on them. In particular, the difficulties people faced in accessing sufficient legitimate income streams and necessary services, whether that be through formal employment, welfare payments or a combination of the two, were situated alongside their perceptions and experiences of other illegitimate options available to them. Most clearly visible to those who became embroiled in 'quasi-cuckooing'-type scenarios (Spicer et al. 2020), the initial attractiveness of allowing people access to their home in return for promises of financial reimbursement, free drugs or other economically appealing outcomes was suggested as being intensified due to their reluctance or lack of ability to generate income through other illegitimate means. Speaking about the apparent attraction of such situations and how they could ultimately lead to cuckooing, one outreach worker suggested:

> It's less immediate isn't it? It might fly under the radar a bit and people might not know that it's happening. And so it might feel less of an immediate risk than shoplifting but also, less hard work. You know, going out shoplifting or sex working is a lot of work and it's a lot of kind of graft over

> the day and whatever. Whereas being in your home and having people use your home may not feel like that it actually requires that much work from you.
>
> (Liam, outreach worker)

In comparison to some of the more immediate risks, practical challenges and potential consequences that may come from the stereotypically 'traditional' avenues associated with heroin use such as acquisitive crime and sex work (see Seddon 2006), the proposition of granting someone access to their home was therefore reported to represent a more attractive option to some. Engaging in agreements that, on the face of it, could perhaps be considered similar to more mainstream practices of 'subletting' or permitting access to a 'lodger' was perceived as being a potentially safer and easier alternative. In comparison to, for example, stealing from a shop, burglary or engaging in prostitution, the risks of allowing people to enter their home were considered as being less well recognised or at the very least less proximate. Quoted in Spicer et al. (2020), 'Susie', a female crack cocaine user who had been affected by cuckooing, made this point succinctly:

> That's why I did it because it saved me going out nicking, instead of doing that I had it there.
>
> (Susie, crack user quoted in Spicer et al. 2020, p. 311)

Viewed myopically, why people make certain decisions that put them at risk of cuckooing and associated exploitation can be difficult to understand. It can also be frustrating for professionals who have tried to warn them of the risks and encouraged them to avoid certain actions. Yet an appreciation of how the economic environment shapes these decisions and what alternative choices are available demonstrates that these decisions are not necessarily irrational. Instead, they result from the complex restraints and enablement that are produced by their economic context.

Continuing a thread initially raised in Spicer et al. (2020), engaging with people looking to access homes as part of generating an 'alternative' illegitimate income stream therefore appears to share similar motivations to why some people engage in 'user-dealing', as opposed to other forms of acquisitive crimes. The body of work published by Ross Coomber and Leah Moyle (among others) on this topic is particularly instructive on this point. Scrutinising 'user-dealing' motivations, they make the straightforward observation that engaging in this activity can represent one of few opportunities often available to those who use heroin and crack cocaine to generate income. Yet, importantly, they also note particular features that make user-dealing among this cohort appealing, including their familiarity with the heroin and crack cocaine supply 'field' (Moyle and Coomber 2017), the relative ease with which this work can be undertaken, and a moral objection to 'real crime' alternatives such as shoplifting (Moyle and Coomber 2015). Involving overlapping populations who are simultaneously located within the realm of the illicit drug market, similar arguments seem to hold weight in the context of cuckooing. Agreeing to or being coerced into providing access and use of their home seemingly poses a more attractive option for some. The nature of this constrained choice is fundamentally grounded in their engagement with the wider legitimate and illegitimate economic environments surrounding them that structure their social world (Harding 2020; Moyle 2019).

The drug market ties that bind

The 'common cuckooing scenario' of the occupant being someone who uses drugs and the 'cuckoo' being someone involved in drug supply also seemingly has the capacity to influence the decisions people make and how they might engage with situations that end up turning into cuckooing. With this relationship between users and dealers structured by the nature of the drug market, the roles occupied by these two typical cohorts in cuckooing set-ups were suggested by interviewees to operate as something akin to a subterranean cultural glue that bound them together in this illicit, clandestine economic world. Notably, this was not just down to the more practical motivations seemingly held by some affected occupants based on the perceived benefits of having easier access to a regular drug supply. Instead, it was suggested as operating as a more general affiliation between the two populations, who had shared interests and experiences in successfully engaging with the workings, functions and goals of illicit drug markets. For the cuckooed occupants, their drug use was typically a significant part of their identity and served to structure their lives. During my doctoral fieldwork, I came across many who were quite open, even among police officers, about buying and using heroin multiple times a day (see Spicer 2021b). Similarly, for those doing the cuckooing, being a drug dealer was central to their identity, with their engagement in drug market activity organising how they spent their time and influencing how they viewed the social world around them. The significant organisation and commitment required to manage a successful County Line demonstrates this point (Harding 2020; Mclean et al. 2019; Spicer 2019).

It is important to recognise within the context of the economic environment how both social groups share something of an attachment to this illegitimate economy while simultaneously typically residing at the margins of the mainstream economy. As one interviewee explained:

> Don't get me wrong, I think a lot of the users don't have much time for many of the dealers. Certainly based on some of the stories that people in here have told to me over the years, the things they say, the way they talk about them, there's not always much love lost between them. So I'm not saying that. I mean you've been asking me about cuckooing in this

> [interview] haven't you, so it's far from hunky dory! But there is this, well I don't know best to say it really, but yeah there is this shared language between them if you know what I mean. They know what each other are all about and they both kind of know what each other want. I mean they do kind of rely on each other a bit don't they, really? As much as they might not want to admit it. So I do think that brings them together a bit. It's a bit of an 'us and them' mentality. 'Us' out there using and scoring and selling, the rest of 'them' out there – the professionals, the police, social services and whatever living in a different world.
>
> (Robin, drug service worker)

It is important not to romanticise the relationship between people who use drugs and those engaged in supply. Evidence from other contexts has demonstrated the violence and abuse that drug suppliers can inflict on people who use drugs, often in an attempt to morally distance themselves (Copes et al. 2015). Of course, the very act of cuckooing, along with its attendant harms, demonstrates the extent and seriousness of victimisation that can occur between these two groups (Robinson et al. 2019). Yet, as has been identified in different contexts (e.g. Bourgois 2003b), amid the shared backdrop of exclusion from the legitimate economy and the refuge offered by the illicit drug market, their interdependence, combined with the shared risks they face from the police and others, appears to bind them together. With both social groups spending significant time in, and having their identities shaped by, the subterranean world of the illicit market, cuckooing was facilitated by not only the physical interactions that inevitably occurred between these groups but seemingly also sometimes a wider sense of cultural affinity engendered by shared participation in a social world built on an illicit marketplace located outside of the legitimate economy.

Constraints, resources and actions

As discussed in the opening chapter, a central theoretical tenet of the risk environment framework is the notion of 'structuration', which helps to analyse the structure-agency relationship. The process of how 'quasi-cuckooing'-type scenarios evolve from facilitating initial access to exploitative home takeovers demonstrates the interplay between structure and agency within this particular context. Stressing the 'contingent' nature of causation, rather than being passive actors, those affected by cuckooing actively interact with their economic environment. Just like other social actors in other structural positions, the economic environment simultaneously constrains and enables them. Particularly notable analytically is the capacity of people affected by cuckooing to draw on the resources that are available to them. Because of their structural position, these resources are almost inevitably limited. Yet, importantly, these resources do exist and are seemingly central to the choices people make, the risks they take and the actions they pursue.

One principal resource drawn on by those affected by cuckooing within their economic environment is the home. As a drug service manager put it, when faced with limited employment opportunities and options to engage in legitimate 'work', some of those affected by cuckooing "*find ways to make their home work for them*". However, while drawing on their home as a resource represented a potentially beneficial option, especially in the face of a range of significant restraints and lack of access to other resources, this had the capacity for these structural restraints to become tighter. It is here where the process of becoming cuckooed can be understood as part of a process of structuration.

This recursive process was particularly visible in cases where the actions people affected by cuckooing took within their structural conditions had the unintended consequence of intensifying them. In this sense, the features of the economic environment that produced cuckooing by making people structurally vulnerable were reproduced. For example, regarding housing, faced with both real and perceived barriers to generating sufficient legitimate income, some people allowed others to access their home, using it as one of the few resources available to them. Yet this often led to this resource slipping away from them. One interviewee described how this process could play out:

> I've seen it a few times now, with several people who you would probably call as being victims of cuckooing. They're in these situations, bad situations, you know. And for whatever reasons they haven't reached out for help. Maybe it hasn't felt there for them, I don't know. And they've used their flat to try and earn a bit. To try and get some pennies to rub together. But it never goes to plan – if they even really have a plan, you know. The police get involved, the flat gets raided, all that stuff. And suddenly that sticky situation they were in just got a whole lot stickier.
>
> (Mel, social worker)

The unintended consequence of losing their home as a result of drawing on it as an economic resource could manifest in various ways. Sometimes it could be through formal eviction, with housing associations or private landlords evicting them because of people accessing their home leading to a breach of tenancy. Alternatively, civil actions such as 'closure orders' could be enacted on particular flats through police involvement because of it being identified as being used for drug supply activity and connected to anti-social behaviour. This particular power was often popular among some police officers due to their capacity to be visible manifestations of 'action' being taken against County Lines and in response to local community concerns (see Spicer 2021b).

Of course, beyond these more formal responses, another unintended way that someone could 'lose' their home was via the cuckooing process itself. Several of the interviewees described cases where people had essentially abandoned their flats because of the harsh, exploitative and threatening conditions they were facing within them, having lost any sense of ownership and autonomy in their home. For others, being immersed in the context of having people active in drug supply operating within the immediate confines of their home led to a problematic escalation of their drug use. The case of 'Neil' recounted in Spicer et al. (2020) demonstrates this. He found allowing dealers to use his home a more attractive option than engaging in forms of acquisitive crime. However, the access to drugs led to him losing control of his drug use, which subsequently led to him losing his home. As he discussed:

> "The main thing was, I ended up losing my house and my car, because where there was someone in the other room with drugs all the time, any time I got my dole money, or any money, I'd keep going into the room and just buy it until I was skint. Then, I lunched out the house, the car, everything."
>
> Interviewer: "Right, so having the gear [drugs] in such close proximity was . . . "
>
> "Yes, it was too tempting, I just spent all my money on it, until I ended up on the street."
>
> (Neil, heroin and crack user quoted in Spicer et al. 2020, p. 313)

Whether losing their home through more 'formal' responses to the presence and actions of others within it, or as a result of cuckooing itself, this demonstrates the recursive link between the outcomes of the choices made within structural conditions. While allowing others initial access to their home was seemingly interpreted by some as being less risky, physically demanding or mentally arduous than pursuing other illegitimate means, this often ended up with them immersed in exploitative cuckooing situations where they faced even worse risks and more desperate circumstances. This could include experiencing violence within their homes, being the focus of consistent police attention, being exploited into drug supply activities or being in a constant state of anxiety because of the people using their home (see also Harding 2020). What initially presented as being a preferable way of alleviating their economic situation often instead turned out to be a victimising trap that placed them at the even sharper economic edges of society.

Conclusion

The economic environment plays a central role in producing cuckooing. It has the power to propel people into becoming structurally vulnerable to being cuckooed through their economic marginalisation, organising how and why it occurs. Yet, as demonstrated by the focus placed on 'quasi-cuckooing' throughout this chapter and the processes that can unfold in these types of scenarios (Spicer et al. 2020), notions of economic causality are contingent on how people engage with and shape this environment. On one level, the economic environment provides the immediate, inescapable structural backdrop for the majority of cuckooing cases. Following many risk environment studies, the role of economic inequality is therefore vital to recognise and devote sufficient attention to, especially given that empirical research evidence of who is affected by cuckooing appears consistent with observations regarding the wider unequal distribution of drug-related harms (see Moyle 2019). Yet, to fully understand the role of the economic environment for cuckooing, it is important for analysis to go beyond reductive or simplistic explanations. The role of this environment is arguably best understood when political-economic factors and the associated structural forces and constraints are contextualised in relation to how people engage with, shape and reproduce them. As powerful as the economic environment is for influencing the experiences and outcomes of those affected by cuckooing, the agency of social actors remains present and important.

Structuration theory provides a useful way of thinking about this process, linking the relationship between structure and agency and how this relationship plays out. Such a theoretically informed analysis in the context of political economy has some precedent in this field. The arguments presented in this chapter have parallels with the concept of 'subterranean structuration', which Alex Stevens (2011) put forward as a way of understanding the nature of the drug-crime relationship. Specifically in the context of cuckooing cases, when faced with the problems associated with a lack of economic resources, for some people, their home represents a potential solution as one of the few limited options available to them. When combined with regular exposure to other drug market actors and a lack of desire to pursue other acquisitive means, engagement in situations that may ultimately end up in exploitative cuckooing scenarios can often follow. Yet, because of the exploitative nature of cuckooing and the formal social control mechanisms that are regularly deployed as a response to drug market activity, what might appear to be a way of mitigating economic difficulties may well end up leading to people's resources becoming further diminished and the structural restraints they experience tightened even stronger. Already faced with being marginalised in a harsh, unforgiving economic environment, being cuckooed can make this even worse.

References

Bourgois, P. (2003a) Crack and the political economy of social suffering. *Addiction Research & Theory*. 11 (1), pp. 31–37.

Bourgois, P. (2003b) *In Search of Respect* (2nd edition). Cambridge: Cambridge University Press.

Chambliss, W. (1975) Toward a political economy of crime. *Theory and Society*. 2 (1), pp. 149–170.

Coomber, R. (2006) *Pusher Myths: Re-Assessing the Drug Dealer*. London: Free Association Books.

Copes, H., Hochstetler, A. and Sandberg, S. (2015) Using a narrative framework to understand the drugs and violence nexus. *Criminal Justice Review*. 40 (1), pp. 32–46.

Densley, J. and Stevens, A. (2015) 'We'll show you gang': The subterranean structuration of gang life in London. *Criminology & Criminal Justice*. 15 (1), pp. 102–120.

Glass, T. and McAtee, M. (2006) Behavioral science at the crossroads in public health: Extending horizons, envisioning the future. *Social Science & Medicine*. 62 (7), pp. 1650–1671.

Harding, S. (2020) *County Lines: Exploitation and Drug Dealing among Urban Street Gangs*. Bristol: Policy Press.

Irwin-Rogers, K. (2019) Illicit drug markets, consumer capitalism and the rise of social media: A toxic trap for young people. *Critical Criminology*. 27 (4), pp. 591–610.

Macdonald, S. J., Donovan, C., Clayton, J. and Husband, M. (2022) Becoming cuckooed: Conceptualising the relationship between disability, home takeovers and criminal exploitation. *Disability & Society*. DOI: https://doi.org/10.1080/09687599.2022.2071680

McLean, R., Robinson, G. and Densley, J. A. (2019) *County Lines: Criminal Networks and Evolving Drug Markets in Britain*. London: Springer.

Moyle, L. (2019) Situating vulnerability and exploitation in street-level drug markets: Cuckooing, commuting, and the 'county lines' drug supply model. *Journal of Drug Issues*. 49 (4), pp. 739–755.

Moyle, L. and Coomber, R. (2015) Earning a score: An exploration of the nature and roles of heroin and crack cocaine 'user-dealers'. *British Journal of Criminology*. 55 (3), pp. 534–555.

Moyle, L. and Coomber, R. (2017) Bourdieu on supply: Utilizing the 'theory of practice' to understand complexity and culpability in heroin and crack cocaine user-dealing. *European Journal of Criminology*. 14 (3), pp. 309–328.

Rhodes, T. (2009) Risk environments and drug harms: A social science for harm reduction approach. *International Journal of Drug Policy*. 20 (3), pp. 193–201.

Rhodes, T., Wagner, K., Strathdee, S. A., Shannon, K., Davidson, P. and Bourgois, P. (2012) Structural violence and structural vulnerability within the risk environment: Theoretical and methodological perspectives for a social epidemiology of HIV risk among injection drug users and sex workers. In: P. O'Campo and J. Dunn (eds). *Rethinking Social Epidemiology*. New York: Springer, pp. 205–230.

Robinson, G., McLean, R. and Densley, J. (2019) Working county lines: Child criminal exploitation and illicit drug dealing in Glasgow and Merseyside. *International Journal of Offender Therapy and Comparative Criminology*. 63 (5), pp. 694–711.

Seddon, T. (2006) Drugs, crime and social exclusion: Social context and social theory in British drugs – crime research. *British Journal of Criminology*. 46 (4), pp. 680–703.

Spicer, J. (2019) That's their brand, their business: How police officers are interpreting county lines. *Policing and Society*. 29 (8), pp. 873–866.

Spicer, J. (2021a) Between gang talk and prohibition: The transfer of blame for county lines. *International Journal of Drug Policy*. 87 (1), pp. 29–37.

Spicer, J. (2021b) *Policing County Lines*. London: Palgrave.

Spicer, J., Moyle, L. and Coomber, R. (2020) The variable and evolving nature of 'cuckooing' as a form of criminal exploitation in street level drug markets. *Trends in Organized Crime*. 23 (4), pp. 301–323.

Stevens, A. (2011) *Drugs, Crime and Public Health*. London: Routledge.

Stevens, A. (2019) 'Being human' and the 'moral sidestep' in drug policy: Explaining government inaction on opioid-related deaths in the UK. *Addictive Behaviors*. 90 (1), pp.444–450.

Stevens, A. (2024) *Drug Policy Constellations: The Role of Power and Morality in the Making of Drug Policy in the UK*. Bristol: Policy Press.

van Draanen, J., Jamula, R., Karamouzian, M., Mitra, S. and Richardson, L. (2023) Pathways connecting socioeconomic marginalization and overdose: A qualitative narrative synthesis. *International Journal of Drug Policy*. DOI: https://doi.org/10.1016/j.drugpo.2023.103971

Wincup, E. and Monaghan, M. (2016) Scrounger narratives and dependent drug users: Welfare, workfare and warfare. *Journal of Poverty and Social Justice*. 24 (3), pp. 261–275.

Young, J. (2011) *The Criminological Imagination*. Cambridge: Polity Press.

3 The spaces and places of cuckooing

Cuckooing is intertwined with the concepts of 'space' and 'place'. A physical space representing someone's home must exist in order for it to be taken over by others. Once established as a place of cuckooing (or 'cuckooed nest'), this will also be located within a broader geographical area. These sites must therefore be situated within and understood in reference to their wider location, which will contain various specific features and characteristics of their own. However, just as it is essential for a physical space to exist for cuckooing to occur, different social actors must also have some type of presence within this space. Their relationships to it, what it represents to them and the meanings they imbue on it will differ. As Gieryn (2000, p. 465) has argued, "*Places are doubly constructed: most are built or in some way physically carved out. They are also interpreted, narrated, perceived, felt, understood, and imagined.*" The concept of 'home' and its associated meanings neatly demonstrates this (Easthope 2004). Of course, the very concept of 'home' and all its attendant social and affective features are themselves worthy of particular attention in this analysis of cuckooing.

Drawing on these ideas, this chapter critically considers the diverse role of the physical environment in producing cuckooing. Similar to the previous chapter, while the immediate and wider physical environment and its various features are foregrounded, analytical emphasis is also placed on how people interact with, place meaning on and construct these spaces (see Fitzgerald 2009). This dual focus acknowledges the importance of the immediate physical context to the places where cases of cuckooing occur while considering the micro-level interpretations and deeper underlying social mechanisms of how this drug market harm is produced and shaped by the features of this particular environment.

Inside the homes of others

Perhaps unsurprisingly, given the nature of their exposure to relevant cases, many of the interviewees suggested that the immediate physical environment where cuckooing took place was an important explanatory factor for how and

DOI: 10.4324/9781032705569-3

why it occurred. Certain features of people's homes were considered to play an important role in producing cuckooing or at least make people more vulnerable to being affected. In the criminological literature, there is a wealth of evidence documenting the relationship between the immediate physical environment and crime. The role of the built environment and housing design in influencing why crime occurs in certain places is a good example (see e.g. Armitage 2013). Similarly, in the context of cuckooing, various physical characteristics situated at the micro level of the physical environment where people lived were seen to play an important role in why they may (or may not) be affected.

One regularly commented-on feature of the physical environment relevant to cuckooing was ground-floor flats. These were considered by many of the interviewees as best avoided for placing those considered at risk of being cuckooed, with a disproportionate number of cases seemingly occurring in these locations. Part of the reason proposed for this was how street-level flats were relatively easy to access compared to those situated higher up in buildings. Because of this physical positioning, people seeking out homes to gain access to were considered more able to disturb and engage with those living in residences at street level. It was easier for them to make occupants aware of their presence, engage in intimidating behaviour or generally pester them for entry. As one interviewee involved in the process of placing vulnerable people into housing outlined:

> We try and stay away from them. We've got a few, but if someone wants to get in then they can absolutely terrorise you on the ground floor. Whereas if people are a bit further up then they can't necessarily get in, well at least not as easily, you know. They can't just walk around the back, start banging, or knock on a window, shouting and all that kind of stuff.
>
> (Ben, housing officer)

In addition to ease of entry, ground-floor flats were also suggested as being more attractive to 'cuckoos' because of the ease of exit. Aligning with observations I made during fieldwork (see Spicer 2021a), the ability to create 'alternative' exits, sometimes afforded by a street-level flat, was considered desirable for those who may wish to make a hasty getaway to avoid being caught in possession of weapons, drugs, or simply not wishing to encounter the police (see also Harding 2020). A police officer recounted an experience of responding to a suspected case of cuckooing in her local area where the ground-floor flat she visited afforded the unwanted inhabitants an opportunity to evade her and the housing officer she was with:

> I remember, actually, I had something a bit like it last year when I went over with a guy called [name of professional] from housing to do a joint visit on this woman who lived over on [name of street]. I don't think she's

> there anymore actually. Anyway there had been some calls about her and there were concerns about her, the usual thing, the usual alarm bells going off, warning signs, you know, so we went to visit. And it was just the two of us that went there, just a welfare check. And we'd knocked on the door a couple of times. I tried to call through the door to tell her who we were. And then these two lads came piling out the back on the other side just as she opened up. They were gone pretty quick. So I think they must have had that planned before we showed up, they must have had that planned out as part of being there.
>
> (Laura, police officer)

In addition to street-level locations within the immediate physical environment, other micro-level features of people's homes and the role these played in making cuckooing more likely to occur were considered important. Communal front doors of buildings hosting multiple flats were highlighted as relevant in relation to how and why certain physical spaces were seemingly more prone to cuckooing. Such features have again been focused on more generally in environmental criminology (Jongejan and Woldendorp 2013). Specifically for cuckooing, rather than offering an extra layer of protection as perhaps might be expected, in some contexts, the role of a communal entrance was considered to reduce the ability of some people to control who entered their building. With people's front doors to their own flats often more hidden behind a main communal door, it was suggested that this could make these spaces less 'defensible' (Newman 1973). It could also sometimes make monitoring situations more difficult for various professionals. For those already vulnerable to cuckooing, having two doors rather than one therefore appeared to paradoxically amplify their vulnerability. As one interviewee described:

> We try and have – it's not always possible – places where people have got their own front door. Because if you've got a communal front door, once somebody's in you haven't necessarily got control over the building, you've only got control over your door.
>
> (Tony, housing officer)

My experiences accompanying police officers and other professionals on welfare visits to those considered at risk of cuckooing aligned with this (see Spicer 2021a). The flats we visited that were situated behind a communal door were often easier to gain access to. The police officers regularly made use of the general traffic of people coming in and out of buildings, either by following other residents into the communal areas or by asking them to 'buzz us through', even though in some cases they did not always immediately know exactly who we were or what we were doing. In several cases, reliance on others was not even necessary, with the doors either being left open or, as in one case, being in such a state of disrepair that it did not close properly.

Having breached this threshold, the chance of the resident then opening their front door to the police officers when we were stood outside their flat within the building often appeared more likely, especially when compared to homes where the sole front door entered out onto a main street. The willingness of officers to stand waiting outside these closed doors for longer or speak (and occasionally listen) through them aided this further.

Making a related observation, Harding (2020) highlighted the capacity for initial access to be obtained in some cuckooing cases simply by people following targeted occupants into their flat. Similarly, the experiences of police officers and other practitioners often gaining relatively easy access to the homes of people they were seeking to engage with appeared to mirror the experiences of those seeking access with underhand motives of cuckooing. The places they found easiest to access were often seemingly also the same places that the 'cuckoos' found easiest to access. Important to note in the context of this chapter is the role the features of these physical spaces played in this. Rather than serving as an additional protective shield, the physical feature of a communal door sometimes appeared to operate more as a cloak that provided greater anonymity and other advantages to those seeking to gain access. Somewhat paradoxically, a communal door combined with a front door located in a corridor could therefore sometimes appear as less than the sum of their parts.

The spatial and temporal dimensions of cuckooing

Analysing temporal shifts in drug markets can deepen understanding of why these illicit worlds are organised in the way they are. Where such concerns have been foregrounded, it has typically been in relation to changes in drug market organisation. Shifts in markets from 'open' to 'closed' are a classic example. The adoption of information technologies to connect actors and facilitate sales is another (Søgaard et al. 2019; Aldridge et al. 2018). As discussed in the opening chapter, the 'amplification spiral' that I argue has played out in relation to the responses to cuckooing has a temporal dimension in how responses to cuckooing have developed over time (see Spicer 2021b). Yet, for the purposes of this risk environment analysis, it is within the context of the micro-level physical environment of cuckooing where the importance of recognising temporality within analysis is arguably particularly worthwhile. Combined with an emphasis on the subjectivities and meanings of those affected by cuckooing, integrating this focus into the cuckooing risk environment analysis provides some valuable insights.

The temporal features of the physical environment are especially relevant when attempting to understand why incidents of cuckooing can reoccur in particular physical spaces over time. Several interviewees commented on this phenomenon, recounting how certain flats continued to be places where cuckooing occurred, despite changes in the people who lived there. In short, while the original occupant might have moved somewhere else after experiencing cuckooing, a cyclical process continued, with these spaces remaining somewhere that cuckooing took place. Some of the aforementioned micro-level physical features of these flats, such as ground-floor locations, were proposed as part of the reason for these recurring cycles. Inevitably, shared characteristics and vulnerabilities among the different occupants who lived in them, most notably in relation to their exposure to the illicit drug market, were also relevant. But intriguingly, it was suggested that, through a process that might be understood as 'subterranean place-making', certain flats became known among those active in the local drug markets as potentially suitable 'hosting' venues. Based on their reputations, these places therefore continued to be targeted by those seeking out suitable places to cuckoo, regardless of who their current occupier was. This demonstrates how 'cuckooed nests' become distinct local 'places' imbued with social meaning and symbolism (c.f. Fitzgerald 2009). As one police officer described:

> We've seen it where the word gets out and certain flats just seem to become known among the drug dealers, the County Lines, as a place to go. People know about it because they've used it before, or they know it because other people have been in that flat before. There's a lot of talking that goes on over time. I wouldn't call it gossiping, that's probably not the right word for it, but, it's, well, you know what I'm saying don't you? These places get known.
>
> (Romesh, police officer)

Several of the interviewees suggested that during the process of housing someone who might be vulnerable to cuckooing, this cycle and its apparent capacity to produce cuckooing were not always appreciated or appropriately considered. For example, recounting such an occasion during his time working with someone who had previously been cuckooed, one interviewee recalled:

> I once turned up with a housing provider to a flat viewing and it said something like "you're fucking dead you grass" on the outside of the flat in giant letters, graffitied all on the wall like, you know. And, well, when I see stuff like that it doesn't make me think the previous tenancy ended that well! But they [housing providers] didn't seem to really have given much thought for what that might mean for them moving in.
>
> (Glen, outreach worker)

Fortunately, such apparent ignorance or apathy of some professionals appeared relatively rare. In most situations where recurring cycles of cuckooing manifested in particular places, it appeared less to do with a lack of awareness on behalf of those attempting to house people likely to be vulnerable to cuckooing and far more to do with a lack of alternative local housing options available. A lack of housing availability reported in many areas where the interviewees worked meant that there were very limited choices, if any, of where people could be housed. Despite concerns about the consequences of this being recognised, it was therefore considered by some not to be uncommon for a flat that had become vacant following the fallout of a cuckooing incident to subsequently be occupied by someone who, because of their connection to the drug market or other vulnerabilities, could unfortunately be considered a prime candidate to be cuckooed themselves.

Building on arguments set out regarding the 'amplification spiral' surrounding cuckooing over recent years (Spicer 2021b), this temporal lens demonstrates how, far from the problem being resolved over time, the cycle of its reoccurrence in particular locations can lead to its reproduction. Understood within the risk environment framework, it is features of the physical environment, such as housing, that need to be foregrounded in understanding how cuckooing is (re)produced, with decisions made by professionals about where people live understood within these constraints. These observations have similarities to Pearson's (1987) analysis of how the 'hard-to-let' syndrome, embedded in certain deprived housing estates, played an important role in the heroin epidemics of the 1980s and where they were concentrated. In the contemporary context of cuckooing, the physical environment where people live appears to play a crucial role in producing and reproducing this drug market-related harm. In turn, this raises the capacity for it to affect not only those directly exploited but also wider communities who live in these places.

Subjective space: interpreting the cuckooed home

Temporality is also relevant to understanding how people's evolving interpretations and subjective experiences of their home relate to the process of 'becoming cuckooed' (MacDonald et al. 2022). The concept of 'home' can be understood in diverse ways. Yet it is the very nature of this subjective process of understanding it as both a 'space' and 'place' that is perhaps most important. People's conceptions of their home are bound up in specific practices and feelings, as well as both material and symbolic boundary markers (Mallett 2004). This interpretation and 'meaning-making' (Parsell 2012) regarding the home shines further light on how cuckooing, as a complex, dynamic, and multifaceted exploitative practice, can develop over time.

The poor physical condition of many homes and how their occupants interpreted and interacted with them appeared to play an important role in some cases of cuckooing. This could serve to instigate how and why people became affected. A social worker described one case he had been involved in and how the person he was working with viewed and engaged with the flat that he lived in. This was a complex case, with a range of issues including drug use and mental health conditions playing a role and presenting various challenges in generating an effective response. But underlying this particular case was a sense that the affected man's relationship with the condition of his home played a key role in how and why it ended up being taken over. As the social worker explained:

> The flat was characterised by just being quite sparse and in disrepair. Furniture would come and go quite a lot. He'd say this was something that would bother him, that the paint was peeling, that the place wasn't nice. And it was a real factor of him thinking like, "well if this space was nicer, I'd find it easier to live here" kind of thing, or "I'd feel more protective of it". But I think it kind of fed in his mind, in his narrative of, "What am I doing here? This flat is in terrible condition, I have got nothing to do, I'm staring at the walls, what's going on here? People are taking the piss". I don't know what the right word would be, but those factors would often kind of collide together in the same kind of sentiment.
>
> (Laurence, social worker)

Other examples illustrated similar dynamics regarding the relationship a person affected by cuckooing had with their home. In a different case, a man ultimately lost control of his home after it had been taken over by a County Lines supply network. But leading up to this, there was also a more general, compounding trend of various people using his home and taking his belongings. This led to him losing autonomy, ownership, and control of this space. As the outreach worker exposed to the case described:

> In his flat on a week-to-week basis almost, or certainly month-to-month, it was like there'd be either new or missing things, like the table that was there last week would be gone. The TV would be gone, or there'd be a new table that someone had bought in. That was potentially complicated by the, you know, presenting aspect of the person's behaviour, especially under stress, kind of chucking things out or their own flat, removing flooring, stuff like that. So it might have been them, but there was also this sense that people were either using it as space to dump stuff or take stuff when they were there, that was my impression.
>
> (Liam, outreach worker)

Such cases demonstrate the interplay between the physical condition of the places where cuckooing occurs and the subjective meanings placed on them by those living in these spaces. While their homes were central places in their lives, some of those affected had developed an apathetic or even antagonistic relationship with these spaces prior to being cuckooed. Faced with poor, often visibly deteriorating housing conditions that had little prospect of improvement, their homes were not somewhere they seemingly held much affection for or took pride in. Instead, it was interpreted as symbolic of where they had found themselves in their life and a reminder of their wider social exclusion. This was likely reinforced by the sheer amount of time these people spent in their homes through unemployment (Stevens 2011).

As suggested by the previous interview quotes, an apparent by-product of these negative feelings toward the home was that, for some, the prospect of having other people come into their domestic environment faced less resistance. A lack of concern about who entered their home and their motivations for doing so seemingly translated into reduced feelings of it being 'polluted' (Douglas 1966) by unwanted intruders in the way that those affected by burglary, for example, have reported (Maguire 1980). Similar to the recursive dynamics of drawing on their home as an economic resource outlined in the previous chapter, this literal and metaphorical opening of their door to others typically made their housing condition and subsequent perceptions of it worse. Upon having their home taken over by others and experiencing other harms commonly associated with being 'cuckooed', this could manifest in a downward spiral. With the physical condition of their home deteriorating further and their experiences while in the home becoming increasingly unpleasant, even stronger negative feelings towards this space and their sense of self within it are likely to occur. As several interviewees recalled, in the most extreme cases, this could lead to someone abandoning their home and living on the street.

Cuckoos in the towers

In addition to the micro-level physical features of the places where cuckooing occurred and the associated subjectivities people placed on their 'home' environment, wider physical locations also play a central role in the cuckooing risk environment. Several interviewees cited local tower blocks as places where cuckooing was highly prevalent. Part of the reason suggested for this was how they concentrated economic deprivation, drug market activity and social interactions into particular physical spaces (Briggs 2013). This again mirrors arguments about the nature of the heroin epidemic in the UK and the role that specific housing estates and related policies played in embedding (and spreading) heroin use and supply due to the concentration of populations and resultant social interactions within them (Pearson 1987). Other physical and social features of these buildings were also considered to make cuckooing more likely. A neighbourhood police officer, for example, discussed the challenges her team faced at a local block of flats considered notorious for cuckooing. The tower block's features were suggested to provide a superficial sense of security to those inside, perhaps similar to the previously discussed nature of communal doors. From their outside position attempting to look in, the police also faced difficulties to understand what was going on within this specific physical environment and how to control it. Describing her experience, she suggested:

> Tower blocks you might think would be useful to prevent cuckooing, because they have key card access and then you have your own key to your front door and sometimes you even have keys to the landings on the floors, so you think it's secure. But they just get the fobs off people and then once they're sort of in there, it's really hard to keep track of what's going on, what flats are affected and what's happening. Because from the outside you can't see anything.
>
> (Clara, police officer)

This physical capacity for tower blocks to 'hide' activities within them was suggested as making cuckooing more prevalent. As local places regularly inflected with rumour, fear and uncertainty, the true extent of this is difficult to ascertain (see Girling et al. 1998 for further discussion regarding the significance of place for producing 'crime-related anxiety'). At the very least, however, the tower blocks generated unease among various practitioners that they were unable to fully understand or control what was going on in places that they considered particularly problematic for cuckooing. Such feelings have parallels with the unfurling of the cuckooing 'amplification spiral' (Spicer (2021b), where the material reality of cuckooing cases combine with the anxious perceptions of relevant professionals to create a sense of things getting increasingly worse and necessitating greater responses that might paradoxically amplify the problem even further. Particularly notable here is how the features of these tower blocks appear to directly contribute to this, further demonstrating the complex and multifaceted role of the physical environment.

In comparison to police officers, those practitioners whose roles led them to have more of a day-to-day presence inside local tower blocks and interact regularly with their residents provided insight by noting other common challenges and experiences. Feelings of anonymity and insecurity, combined with a perceived lack of presence of 'capable guardians' (Hollis et al. 2013), created a sense among residents that scenarios like cuckooing were something that regularly occurred yet were rarely responded to appropriately or swiftly. As one housing officer discussed:

> In a multi-story, people will often come up and say to us "oh we never see our housing officer in here, why aren't you doing anything about so and so down the hall?". Well, actually we've been in that block, you know, three times at that particular week. But all they've got is a spy hole to look into the hallways; that's all they've got, so they won't necessarily see us.
>
> (Alyssa, housing officer)

These feelings were made more complex given that these tower blocks were places where more general drug market activity, antisocial behaviour, disruptive tenants and unwelcome visitors were not uncommon and could often be visible (see Foster 2000). Consequently, when cuckooing cases did occur in these locations, these exploitative scenarios were sometimes not recognised for what they were. Instead, they were interpreted by a range of stakeholders, including other residents and some practitioners, as being more akin to a 'crack house' set-up or similar type of antisocial, criminogenic space (Briggs 2010). Several of the interviewees suggested that an unfortunate result of this was that the exploitative, messy realities of these cases and the complex vulnerabilities of those affected could be overlooked (see also Macdonald et al. 2022). A drug service manager, for example, drew on the experiences of several of her service users to outline how cases of cuckooing could become subsumed into more general venues associated with drug use, supply and antisocial behaviour if taking place in tower blocks where these were regular occurrences. As she explained:

> Where there's 'crack houses' or 'using flats' or 'squats', those types of places, it's quite difficult to tell the difference between that and a 'cuckooed flat'. If people are coming and going all the time, you know. And it's a bit of a kind of grey area anyway I guess. So places where that's more the norm are less likely to be picked up and seen.
>
> (Beth, drug service manager)

Of course, misidentifying cuckooing scenarios as 'crack houses' is not unique to tower blocks. Despite the amount of awareness raising that has occurred over recent years, overlooking the exploitative dynamics of cuckooing remains far from an unheard-of occurrence more generally, regardless of location (see Moyle 2019; Spicer 2021a). But because of the wider social milieu connected with the drug market that is often (re)produced within tower blocks, and the general problems associated with and experienced in these physical environments, it appears that there is often a greater chance of the exploitative nature of cuckooing scenarios being overlooked when they occurred in these locations. Not only do the physical features of these tower blocks therefore appear to make some people more vulnerable to cuckooing, but this is also bound up with them as social spaces, which influence interpretations of what constitutes a genuine case of cuckooing and how to respond.

This point was demonstrated further in relation to how some people working in these tower blocks had reacted to certain cases of cuckooing when they had occurred. One interviewee, for example, suggested that the heightened attention, awareness-raising, and sometimes alarmist warnings about cuckooing appeared to have had the unfortunate effect of striking fear into some housing providers. This had then resulted into them jumping into rushed responses, with the outcomes often being unhelpful, counterproductive or punitive to those affected. As he discussed:

> I think with other landlords I've struggled a bit and people have got in a bit of a panic. Because although generally, council housing officers have a lot of experience of people with issues and drugs and stuff, I think cuckooing you know, as a term, scares the crap out of people. So, we've struggled a bit in the past, people have, people, I think housing officers in the past have been too punitive and come in and not stopped for a second and thought: what's going on here? how can we unpack this? how can we take it forward?
>
> (Glen, outreach worker)

The interpretations, meanings and 'place-making' associated with 'homes' therefore appear far from something that only concerns those directly affected by cuckooing but also seem to play an important role with responders.

Location, location, location

The start of this chapter focused on various micro-level features of the physical environment that play a role in producing cuckooing before moving into considering the case of tower blocks that sit more at the meso-level. At this point, it is worth widening the lens further to consider macro-level features. Of note are the geographic locations of towns and cities. Combined with their specific features, their locations appear to play an important role in how and why cuckooing manifests. This was driven by the organisation of the local heroin and crack cocaine market in certain areas, itself dictated by the macro physical environment, and was suggested as significantly influencing the amount and nature of cuckooing that took place.

Demonstrating this, one town understood to be structured predominantly as a 'secondary' drug market to a nearby city was considered to have a relatively minimal presence of 'out-of-town' dealers, who are typically the principal undertakers of cuckooing (Coomber and Moyle 2018). Instead, in the opposite of a County Lines drug supply methodology, the drug market for this town was reported to be made up predominantly of local dealers and the types of user-dealers that Moyle and Coomber (2015) have termed 'nominated buyers', who travel to the nearby city and then return to the local area to buy for themselves as well as to sell within their local networks. As one interviewee discussed:

> There's not a lot of outside gangs like you have in other areas. I mean [name of town] being a secondary market and the same with [name of different town] means that you've got local people going to purchase drugs off [name of major city] based dealers to then take back into a secondary

> market. So we don't have a lot of local dealers mimicking County Lines models.
>
> (Seth, drug service manager)

Despite not being immune to cuckooing, whether that be through the occasional presence of County Line suppliers or forms of 'local' cuckooing (Spicer et al. 2020), incidences were described as less common because of this town's drug market structure and how it organised supply activities.

In comparison, areas reported as having their retail-level supply of heroin and crack cocaine dominated by County Lines networks reported more cases, with 'out-of-town' dealers seeking out places to stay while located in the area. Following arguments made elsewhere (see Coomber 2015), geographical location therefore plays an important role in interacting with and shaping the organisation of local drug markets. It influences both how drug supply activity is structured and ultimately what takes place within it as a specific social and transactional milieu.

The role of the macro-physical environment, its influence on drug market organisation and its role in producing cuckooing can be deepened by drawing on various existing insights from the drug market literature. Reuter and MacCoun's (1992) somewhat forgotten 'distance-travelled typology' of retail drug markets provides a relevant analytic device. So-called 'export' markets, where people who use drugs travel to physical drug market locations away from their immediate locale to purchase them, represent perhaps the least susceptible retail drug market type to cuckooing. Conversely, markets termed as 'import', where the supplier travels to a foreign locale to sell to local customers, represent the most susceptible. So-called 'local' markets appear to sit somewhere in between. Concepts such as rurality also inevitably play a role here, feeding into local drug culture and associated market dynamics (Copes et al. 2015). But the central point for the purposes of this analysis is that the geographical location and features of a town or city fundamentally matter when it comes to understanding the production of cuckooing. This stresses the continued importance of remembering that drug markets are not the same, despite often being discussed in homogenised ways (Coomber 2006). Their harms and capacity for violence and forms of exploitation such as cuckooing can vary, often significantly. Appreciating this further deepens understanding of why, how and where cuckooing occurs.

Conclusion

At the micro, meso and macro levels, the physical environment comprises an important part of the cuckooing risk environment. To return to observations made at the start of this chapter regarding the essential components of cuckooing, it would perhaps be impossible for it not to. Taking what the practice of 'cuckooing' must involve as an analytic starting point stresses the role(s) played by the physical environment in understanding how and why this practice occurs. The various physical features of where people live, including communal doors or street-level flats, that appear to play a role in making cuckooing more likely demonstrate this. Situating places where cuckooing occurs within wider geographic locations, whether that be the tower block in which a flat is located or the town where someone lives, also shows how various features of the physical environment set the contextual stage for cuckooing to play out. As the Chicago School theorists stressed over a century ago, there is value in scrutinising the role of the physical environment when attempting to understand why certain types of crime occur within certain social milieus hosted by certain places.

In one sense, the physical environment is therefore essential to the cuckooing risk environment as this drug market-related harm has a distinct and unavoidable material reality. But crucially, this is only part of the story when it comes to the physical environment. As stressed throughout this chapter, the places where cuckooing occurs are also socially 'made'. A range of actors invest them with values and ascribe them different meanings. This includes the affected person's interpretation of their home before, during and after being cuckooed, the sense of risk and security that those taking over homes might have about certain potential target sites, the narratives about places that are (re)produced among communities and how practitioners interpret the places of cuckooing that they come across. All these serve to construct the places where cuckooing occurs just as much as the bricks and mortar used to make up the walls that surround them. Scrutinising both the physical and social conceptions of people's homes is therefore fundamentally important for understanding how and why cuckooing occurs in the places it does.

References

Aldridge, J., Stevens, A. and Barratt, M. J. (2018) Will growth in cryptomarket drug buying increase the harms of illicit drugs? *Addiction*. 113 (5), pp. 789–796.

Armitage, R. (2013) *Crime Prevention Through Housing Design: Policy and Practice*. London: Springer.

Bacon, M. and Spicer, J. (2023) Harm reduction policing: Conceptualisation and implementation. In: M. Bacon and J. Spicer (eds). *Drug Law Enforcement, Policing and Harm Reduction: Ending the Stalemate*. London: Routledge, pp. 13–38.

Briggs, D. (2010) Crack houses in the UK: Some observations on their operations. *Drugs and Alcohol Today*. 10 (4), pp. 33–42.

Briggs, D. (2013) *Crack Cocaine Users: High Society and Low Life in South London*. London: Routledge.

Coomber, R. (2006) *Pusher Myths: Re-Assessing the Drug Dealer*. London: Free Association Books.

Coomber, R. (2015) A tale of two cities: Understanding differences in levels of heroin/crack market-related violence – A two city comparison. *Criminal Justice Review*. 40 (1), pp. 7–31.

Coomber, R. and Moyle, L. (2018) The changing shape of street-level heroin and crack supply in England: Commuting, holidaying and cuckooing drug dealers across 'county lines'. *British Journal of Criminology*. 58 (6), pp. 1323–1342.

Copes, H., Hochstetler, A. and Sandberg, S. (2015) Using a narrative framework to understand the drugs and violence nexus. *Criminal Justice Review*. 40 (1), pp. 32–46.

Douglas, M. (1966) *Purity and Danger*. London: Routledge and Kegan Paul.

Easthope, H. (2004) A place called home. *Housing, Theory and Society*. 21 (3), pp. 128–138.

Fitzgerald, J. L. (2009) Mapping the experience of drug dealing risk environments: An ethnographic case study. *International Journal of Drug Policy*. 20 (3), pp. 261–269.

Foster, J. (2000) Social exclusion, crime and drugs. *Drugs: Education, Prevention and Policy*. 7 (4), pp. 317–330.

Gieryn, T. F. (2000) A space for place in sociology. *Annual Review of Sociology*. 26 (1), pp. 463–496.

Girling, E., Loader, I. and Sparks, R. (1998) A telling tale: A case of vigilantism and its aftermath in an English town. *British Journal of Sociology*. 49 (3), pp. 474–490.

Harding, S. (2020) *County Lines: Exploitation and Drug Dealing among Urban Street Gangs*. Bristol: Policy Press.

Hollis, M. E., Felson, M. and Welsh, B. C. (2013) The capable guardian in routine activities theory: A theoretical and conceptual reappraisal. *Crime Prevention and Community Safety*. 15 (1), pp. 65–79.

Jongejan, A. and Woldendorp, T. (2013) A successful CPTED approach: The Dutch 'police label secure housing'. *Built Environment*. 39 (1), pp. 31–48.

Macdonald, S. J., Donovan, C., Clayton, J. and Husband, M. (2022) Becoming cuckooed: Conceptualising the relationship between disability, home takeovers and criminal exploitation. *Disability & Society*. DOI: https://doi.org/10.1080/09687599.2022.2071680

Maguire, M. (1980) The impact of burglary upon victims. *British Journal of Criminology*. 20 (1), pp. 261–275.

Mallett, S. (2004) Understanding home: A critical review of the literature. *The Sociological Review*. 52 (1), pp. 62–89.

Moyle, L. (2019) Situating vulnerability and exploitation in street-level drug markets: Cuckooing, commuting, and the 'county lines' drug supply model. *Journal of Drug Issues*. 49 (4), pp. 739–755.

Moyle, L. and Coomber, R. (2015) Earning a score: An exploration of the nature and roles of heroin and crack cocaine 'user-dealers'. *British Journal of Criminology*. 55 (3), pp. 534–555.

Newman, O. (1973) *Defensible Space*. London: Architectural Press.

Parsell, C. (2012) Home is where the house is: The meaning of home for people sleeping rough. *Housing Studies*. 27 (2), pp. 159–173.

Pearson, G. (1987) Social deprivation, unemployment and patterns of heroin use. In N. Dorn and N. South (eds). *A Land Fit for Heroin?* London: Palgrave, pp. 62–94.

Reuter, P. and MacCoun, R. J. (1992) Street drug markets and inner-city neighbourhoods: Matching policy to reality. In J. B. Steinberg, D. W. Lyon and M. E. Vaiana (eds). *Urban America: Policy Choices for Los Angeles and the Nation.* Santa Monica: Rand Corporation, pp. 227–251.

Søgaard, T. F., Kolind, T., Haller, M. B. and Hunt, G. (2019) Ring and bring drug services: Delivery dealing and the social life of a drug phone. *International Journal of Drug Policy.* 69 (1), pp. 8–15.

Spicer, J., Moyle, L. and Coomber, R. (2020) The variable and evolving nature of 'cuckooing' as a form of criminal exploitation in street level drug markets. *Trends in Organized Crime.* 23 (4), pp. 301–323.

Spicer, J. (2021a) *Policing County Lines.* London: Palgrave.

Spicer, J. (2021b) The policing of cuckooing in 'county lines' drug dealing: An ethnographic study of an amplification spiral. *The British Journal of Criminology.* 61 (5), pp. 1390–1406.

Stevens, A. (2011) *Drugs, Crime and Public Health.* London: Routledge.

4 Cuckooing and drug policy choices

The previous two chapters have taken relatively broad sweeps of the economic and physical environments, and their relevant micro- and macro-level features. Drawing on structuration theory, both also placed analytic attention on the agency of those who become affected by cuckooing and how human action can reproduce the structural conditions people are in. This chapter continues this approach by considering the role of the policy environment (Rhodes (2002). However, it differs slightly from the previous two chapters in that its attention is placed firmly on one particular aspect of this environment in the form of drug policy. Alex Stevens (2017, p. 826) defines drug policy as being the "laws, decisions, funding programmes, and instructions by which the state affects discourses and practices on illicit drugs". In addition to questions surrounding legality, drug policy therefore encapsulates a range of other areas and political choices (see Ritter 2022 for an excellent overview). Shaped by ethico-political "constellations" (Stevens 2024), these diverse areas combine to produce the drug policy environment and its outcomes. Accordingly, many of these drug policy features play an important role in relation to cuckooing.

A specific focus on drug policy is necessary, given that, while not exclusively a practice located within drug markets and involving their actors (see Macdonald et al. 2022), it is the understanding of cuckooing as a drug market-related harm that is the specific focus of this book. To address the role of UK drug policy in producing structural vulnerability to cuckooing, three broad yet fundamental areas of this policy domain are addressed. These are drug prohibition and illicit markets; the criminalisation of drug possession; and trends in drug treatment. Serving to structure the chapter, the analysis of each of these drug policy areas provides insight into how vulnerability to cuckooing is produced by structural features and related factors that exist externally to those affected. As part of this, attention is given to contrasting policy proposals that sit in opposition to current drug policy. In turn, the discussions and arguments put forward naturally lead to considering what an enabling environment for reducing cuckooing harms might look like.

DOI: 10.4324/9781032705569-4

Cuckooing and drug prohibition: addressing the illicit market

The thorny question of whether to 'legalise drugs' is regularly raised in the drug field. Such policy deliberation is nothing particularly new. As long as prohibitionist policies have existed, so too have counterarguments about the merits of pursuing an alternative direction when standing at the regulatory crossroads of how to 'control' drugs (Seddon 2020a). Those who have traced these debates historically have identified how calls for legalisation have emanated from a range of stakeholders and interest groups (e.g. Seddon 2020b). In recent years, this plurality of voices has perhaps become even louder, and its speakers more visible, with an apparent upsurge in more general awareness of drug policy reform among the public. One contributing factor for this has been the emergence of legalisation policies across various international jurisdictions, including the introduction of legal cannabis vendors in Canada and various states in the US, which are now playing out in practice. Within the UK, the work of organisations concerned with drug policy reform, such as Transform Drug Policy Foundation, Release, and Volteface, combined with the burgeoning profiles of various outspoken critics of the so-called 'war on drugs' (e.g. Woods 2016), has also served to elevate this more prominently onto the public consciousness (Stevens 2024).

Though sometimes generating more heat than light, the 'legalisation debate' and associated arguments have typically centred on the fundamental reasons why drug-related problems exist and how best to respond to them (MacCoun and Reuter 2001). With cuckooing understood as a drug market-related harm, this becomes specifically relevant in the context of this study. It is therefore also unsurprising that certain levels of consciousness regarding legalisation arguments were prominent in the minds of some interviewees. When considering the policy environment for cuckooing and the role this played in producing structural vulnerability to people being affected, the apparent failures of a drug policy rooted in prohibitionist principles and the possible benefits of moving towards a legally regulated drug market were often voiced.

Various interviewees raised the policy proposal of drug legalisation. They also discussed this with different levels of detail and knowledge. For some, this involved little more than a desire to point out the apparent failures of prohibition, with legalisation – albeit often not particularly well defined – proposed in a binary sense against the current criminal justice-orientated system. Following this dichotomy, notions of 'legalisation' represented *the* alternative drug policy option to what is currently in place. The following quote from a drug service worker demonstrates such thinking:

> I think my take on it is something like this. This isn't the official position of [name of drug service] or anything so don't go thinking that, right. But

> with drugs policy and all that, well let's look at what's happening now. Basically we've been trying this stuff of 'just say no' and all that crap for years and years. And is it working? Well no, not really. People are still doing it. You've got all the County Lines, the exploitation, the grooming, the cuckooing that we're talking about and all that. So I say – and it's not just me saying this, you know – I say let's try the different approach. Let's legalise it, let's tax it and see what happens.
>
> (Simon, drug service worker)

From this viewpoint, cuckooing represents a further symptom of a failing prohibitionist drug policy. Situated alongside other drug-related harms, its existence therefore becomes an additional reason to pursue a fundamental change in direction through a policy U-turn.

Other interviewees went into more detail, discussing the underlying mechanisms generated within the prohibitionist drug policy environment that had a role in producing vulnerability to cuckooing. In turn, the potential benefits of legalisation in relation to this area and how a legally regulated market might serve to combat this were defined. Understanding cuckooing as an exploitative practice not just located in, but also produced by, the illicit drug market, the social interactions that took place between different market actors were considered central to how and why it occurred. The attractiveness of drug legalisation for several interviewees in the context of cuckooing was that it represented a way of cutting the social ties between people who use drugs and illicit dealers. Under the type of regulatory models proposed by Transform (2009), it was suggested that people who use drugs would not need to engage with or be exposed to illicit dealers. Within this 'imagined' alternative drug policy environment (Wakeman 2014), the existence of illicit dealers would therefore severely diminish. Accordingly, so too would the practice of cuckooing. As one police officer, who had been outspoken about their views on drug policy reform when I had spent time with them previously during a shift, outlined:

> Well you already know my thoughts about drug policy and how I think that would help. We've talked about that before when you came out with us. Because when it comes down to it, the main vulnerability in my eyes is that they're drug addicts and they have to buy Class A. And so they come into contact with these dealers that they can't avoid not coming into contact with 'cause they've got to buy the drugs. And then, well you know, it all leads on from there.
>
> (Clara, police officer)

Demonstrating an interesting integration of drug legalisation arguments within contemporary policing concerns about vulnerability (Keay and Kirby 2018), in this sense, people's vulnerability to cuckooing was viewed as being produced by the existence of the illicit drug market and their exposure to it. This argument has resonance with Goldstein's (1985) influential notion of 'systemic' drug-related violence. Put simply, this explanation for drug market violence rests on the contention that, being an unregulated social arena, their actors do not have access to formal conflict resolution. The use of violence becomes the preferred, perhaps even inevitable way that disputes are settled, while the illicit nature of the market fosters violent predation and retaliation (Jacques and Allen 2015). In the context of cuckooing, the nature of the drug market as a social space operating outside of formal legal channels similarly appears to provide an important policy generated context. Not only does the prohibitionist policy context create the illicit market in which different actors engage, but it also exposes these different actors to each other to create harmful externalities that exist beyond the basic market dynamic of exchanges. Cuckooing represents one of these externalities. Though not strictly necessary in the context of the basic exchanges that make up the totality of the illicit drug market, it is nonetheless a practice that is seemingly produced as part of the wider social milieu grounded in the policy environment of prohibition. Understood in this way, prohibition therefore represents a mechanism of this harm, with alternative forms of regulation representing a suitable alternative and potentially transformative intervention.

Criminalising drug possession

The critique of drug prohibition and the nature of associated 'legalisation' policy proposals typically reside at the level of the drug market, with the basic premise resting on the desire to lift illicit supply out of the darkness of the underground criminal enterprise and into the enlightened conditions attributed to a legally regulated system. A slightly different area of drug policy concerns the criminal sanctions given to people caught in possession of illicit drugs. Accordingly, different drug policy proposals are associated aligning broadly with the notion of 'decriminalisation' (Stevens et al. 2022). Being the site of an apparent 'quiet revolution' internationally (Eastwood et al. 2016), this was a policy area less explicitly referred to by the interviewees. Yet, often implicitly, the notion of criminalising people who use drugs and the role this played in cases of cuckooing was often raised. This then stressed a further important feature of the cuckooing risk environment, located in the domain of drug policy.

Building on previous observations (see Spicer 2021), central to this was how people's experiences of being criminalised for drug possession – or at least their awareness of the threat of it – could hamper the process of them being identified and responded to as a victim of cuckooing. This policy-generated context played out in multiple ways. At one level, it related to the capacity for their victimhood to not be recognised and appropriately responded to by the police and other practitioners because of the presence of drug possession offending. At another level, it meant that those affected by cuckooing whose identity was 'totalised' by their drug use were less inclined to cooperate with safeguarding responses. In short, the policy of criminalising possession of illicit drugs was seen to make many people who were vulnerable to cuckooing unwilling to engage with police officers, as well as some other related practitioners in their apparent efforts to identify them as victims and respond accordingly.

Such observations have similarities to other consequences of the criminalisation agenda of drug policy identified in various studies focused on drug-related harms, such as being hesitant to call emergency services at the scene of an overdose (Moore and Dietze 2005). Specifically in the context of cuckooing, the barrier that criminalisation represented to engagement was considered problematic for various reasons. One was how it risked significantly limiting the extent and nature of the safeguarding measures that professionals attempted to implement when someone was considered either at risk of being cuckooed or currently being affected. Simultaneously, it was also considered to negatively affect how these measures were interpreted and ultimately received by the intended recipients (see Spicer 2021). With the drug policy-generated context of criminalisation looming large over both parties and shaping the nature of their interactions, trust and collaboration could be in short supply. Various examples were given of how this core drug policy feature fed into the micro-level interactions between practitioners and people vulnerable to cuckooing. These interactions were identified across various professionals, demonstrating the power that runs throughout the various systems that people who use drugs encounter (Bacon and Seddon 2020). Perhaps somewhat inevitably, however, it was the work of the police and specific experiences of arrests for drug offences where this was most prevalent.

Illustrating this, a drug worker discussed a case involving a woman previously engaged in a treatment programme at his service. She had suffered a particularly nasty episode of cuckooing in her flat at the hands of a network of 'out of town' dealers, which included experiences of sadistic violence and serious sexual assaults. Amid this situation, she had also been arrested for drug possession offences, which came on top of several other similar previous convictions. Following the most recent arrest and subsequent criminal proceedings, her engagement with the drug service began to wane. Relatedly, the identification of her as an 'offender' also undermined efforts to recognise the victimisation and exploitation she had received through the cuckooing situation. The drug service worker explained his frustration:

> But we can't really help them if the police nick them. When they're like, "Right, put the braces on, off you go". And I understand why. I get it. I understand. You know, society wants their pound of flesh. But then often they take the pound of flesh out of the person that's got the least flesh to give. And that's where it becomes difficult for us as agencies and workers,

> because we then have to go, "Look, we understand what the government policies are, blah, blah, blah, that's all black-and-white, written on paper, but I've got a person standing in front of me who's been cuckooed, has been bitten, has been raped. Ok so they're in possession of crack I know there are things you have to do about that but what are we doing about what really matters here?"
>
> (Simon, drug service worker)

The impact of criminalising drug possession is one example of how an 'offender' identity could seemingly undermine attempts to suitably recognise and respond to people affected by cuckooing. Alongside this, the messy, complex reality of those engaging in 'user-dealing' and their criminalisation is also relevant in this policy environment context. While Chapter 2 highlighted how engaging in 'quasi-cuckooing' (Spicer et al. 2020) set-ups can represent an attractive alternative means of generating income, it is also important to recognise that many who become cuckooed also end up engaging more explicitly in user-dealing activities as part of these scenarios, perhaps having had experience of being involved in supply before (see Moyle 2019). Engaging in low-level supply activity might be through a certain level of constrained choice, with further rewards being on offer for undertaking this work on behalf of the suppliers residing in their home. Alternatively, in some cases, taking on the role and responsibilities of being a 'runner' may be better understood as being forced upon them by dealers as part of the wider exploitative dynamics commonly attributed to County Lines drug supply (Coomber and Moyle 2018). Regardless of the exact nature of the user-dealing situation, the role of the drug policy environment is demonstrated at the point where someone being cuckooed and undertaking supply-related 'running' activities is arrested by the police. In such cases, the arrest and subsequent consequences can seemingly make some more vulnerable, both in a general sense and within the specific context of the cuckooing situation they are embroiled in.

In particular, the consequences of such arrests in the form of having drugs and/or money seized from them can generate a situation where people are put at greater risk of harm and may end up further entangled in both a cuckooing scenario and related exploitation (see Bacon 2016 for broader observations regarding arrests of this population). Speaking about this, one police sergeant was candid in sharing the concerns she had about what the effect of such arrests could be and how pursuing these law enforcement activities grounded in the criminalisation-oriented drug policy context could generate harm. As she discussed:

> The risk is really high. And also I mean I've been in those anxious positions where you've taken drugs off somebody who is a user-dealer and you know that they are going to get beaten up for that. So having that understanding of exactly what position we are putting those people in is

> really, really important. It is a bloody horrible place to be lying there in the middle of the night thinking 'oh my god I didn't do the safeguarding for this person or that.' You know we need to understand what we are dealing with because it is people's lives. I know that the cuckooing, the victim is – I mean the ultimate risk is death – but the likelihood is it's more threats and intimidation and maybe being beaten up so it is so sort of physical harm. Like it might be a black eye or you know other beatings that they will never tell anyone about. But understanding that risk is there and the part we play in it is really, really important.
>
> (Jean, police sergeant)

Recognising the potentially detrimental impact of arrests is notable, especially given how it appears to undermine claims that the policing of this area is grounded in recognising exploitation, reducing vulnerabilities and safeguarding those at risk of cuckooing and related harms (Coliandris 2015). Following her open reflections of the role the police can play in implementing core aspects of the policy environment, this officer then went on to consider what alternative options could be pursued. Her comments are revealing of the role played by the drug policy environment and the constraints it creates:

> And I don't know what the answer is other than, you know, by arresting them sometimes they are in a place of safety. But the reality is they are going to be caught up with in a matter of days. I don't know what the solution is for that because that is the tricky area when somebody has become complicit in the problem and they are the easy focus. You know you get somebody, the way we catch drug dealers is to target the person who is dealing and more often than not now that is the person going out on the street who is already the victim. I don't know what the solution is. I think the sensible idea would be that you don't take the drugs and you don't take the money. But that is not a realistic option is it?
>
> (Jean, police sergeant)

Perhaps most notable in these reflections is that, despite recognising that law enforcement actions can generate harm and having a desire to avoid this, changes that might allow this to occur appear at best difficult and at worse impossible within the existing policy context. As 'street level bureaucrats' (Lipsky 1980), police officers possess significant capacity for discretion in how they undertake their work and implement policy on the ground. Yet, in this case, the 'law on the books' in the form of current drug policy seemingly remains too much of a straitjacket at times for these harms to be avoided. Instead, rooted in prohibitionist principles and a criminalisation agenda, the existing drug policy environment seems to play a central, multifaceted role in generating some of the harms that those affected by cuckooing experience and undermining desires to reduce them.

Drug treatment: addressing heroin and crack use

The previous two sections of this chapter have concentrated on the 'criminalising' features of UK drug policy and the involvement of the criminal justice system in shaping this policy environment. However, as outlined at the start of the chapter, it is important to recognise that the field of drug policy is broad in scope and spans far beyond concerns about legality, prohibition and enforcement (Ritter 2022). One further area of the drug policy environment related to cuckooing raised by various interviewees was the nature of the drug treatment system in the UK. Critical attention was specifically placed on changes that have occurred in this field over the last decade or so, and the ramifications relevant to cuckooing.

As detailed in the Black Review commissioned by the UK government (Black 2021), significant reductions in funding to drug treatment during the wider period of economic austerity since 2010 led to a stark reduction of services. Both in the overall capacity of treatment provision and in the quality of what was provided, these policy choices led to reductions in resources that have significantly hampered the ability of services and the people who work within them (Winstock et al. 2021). Coinciding with this reduction in drug treatment funding over the last decade has been an ideological turn towards 'recovery' and abstinence, illustrated by the emphasis on so-called 'recovery completion' as the desired outcome of drug treatment engagement. Part of the consequences of this has been a reduction in harm reduction measures (Stevens 2022). Particularly relevant in relation to cuckooing is how this combination of funding reductions and recovery orientation has seemingly led to challenges in generating treatment engagement among the heroin and/or crack cocaine using cohort (Winstock et al. 2021).

As one drug service manager suggested, because of this, while the overall numbers of people who use these drugs may not have changed significantly over this time period, the number of those not engaged in treatment – at least in a consistent and meaningful way – seemingly has. Among other things, this has potentially significant implications for their engagement with illicit markets. As he outlined in detail:

> I think one of the one of my issues is the recovery agenda over the last 10 years. It's meant that fewer and fewer people seem to find the treatment systems on offer. And they don't find the services as acceptable or accessible. We've got fewer and fewer opium and crack users accessing services and opiate use especially. And whether that opens up markets . . . well it's hard to see how it doesn't isn't it? But the fact that numbers in treatment are going down or the throughput of opiate users, especially those dropping out is increasing, then the demand for opiates increases. Because if you look at how NDTMS [National Drug Treatment Monitoring System] report stuff – and bearing in mind the NDTMS has a political function to

> keep the people that hold the purse strings happy – is that if you just look at unmet need in a given year, what proportion of the estimated opiate users are in treatment? You know it might say that 50% of the estimated opiate users in a given area are being in treatment. Well, what that's not telling you is that any one time it might only be 30%, and then there's a huge throughput and it's not effective in treatment, it's not effective. So that means there's more people in the community relying on the illicit opioid market which drives up the demand for drugs. So I think that that creates an environment where a County Lines model can thrive because, you know there's more, there's a bigger market to serve.
>
> (Seth, drug service manager)

In short, the more heroin and crack cocaine users not engaged with treatment, the more likely it is that there will be a greater use of these illicit drugs, and therefore more demand on illicit supply. This, in turn, is likely to create more thriving illicit drug markets. The capacity for these markets to become more firmly entrenched in communities may make cuckooing more likely to occur (Harding 2020). The related capacity for such markets to evolve and develop, particularly in relation to the greater presence of County Lines networks in more provincial areas that has been observed over recent years, has the potential to make cuckooing even more prevalent (see Robinson et al. 2019).

Alongside the negative consequences stemming from the political choices that have impacted the drug treatment field and wider drug policy environment over the last decade, there was a backdrop of frustration felt by some of the interviewees about the nature of the drug treatment system and how it managed people engaged with it. A particular aspect of this related to the provision of opiate substitution therapy (OST). Experiences of being prescribed methadone or buprenorphine could be challenging, representing an often-bumpy treatment journey. Of course, the complex nature of drug dependence and drug treatment means that certain challenges and bumps in the road are to be expected (see Harris and McElrath 2012). But the nature of the policy environment seemingly played a central role in exacerbating these experiences and the negative repercussions. Its 'recovery' orientation sometimes seemingly incentivised premature OST cessation and facilitated punitive sanctions to those who did not fully comply with the associated requirements while engaging with a treatment programme. As one interviewee lamented:

> Oh god, the countless times one of my clients actually went off script because, I don't know, something happened to them. Yeah, and they can have like a bad day or whatever, we all can, but if you don't go for three days, if you don't pick up your script and do what you need to do, that's it, you're out. And then you have to through all of this interview process

> again, you have to be lucky enough that there is somebody available, and compete with a load of bla, bla, bla bullshit.
>
> (Pam, outreach worker)

In the context of cuckooing, such observations are important given that people who use heroin and may therefore be engaged with OST appear to make up the main cohort affected by this exploitative drug market practice (Coomber and Moyle 2018; Harding 2020; Moyle 2019; Spicer et al. 2020). Following these observations about the role of the drug policy environment in influencing this cohort's engagement with treatment, there appear to be some significant implications for the role of this policy environment in producing vulnerability to cuckooing. One main implication is that, at an individual level, not being engaged in treatment can lead to people becoming involved with the illicit heroin and crack market or at least becoming involved in it more often than they already do. As discussed earlier in this chapter, interactions with actors within illicit drug markets can lead to people becoming exposed to dealers seeking out homes to take over. By not being engaged with treatment and facing the various challenges associated with sustaining regular heroin and/or crack cocaine use, the lure of allowing access to their home as a way of achieving this can often be strong. As one interviewee outlined, in this situation, the value of simply telling someone not to let others into their home was unlikely to be particularly effective:

> It's not practical. So, I used to have a client, he had a tenancy where you can't let visitors in, and he's at risk of losing his tenancy if he did. I had a really interesting chat, bless him, I'd only met him for about an hour or so. We were just towards the end of a chat and we were just talking about cuckooing and that. I said "look, what can we do to help you manage your door?". He said "I'll be honest mate, nothing. If somebody tells me they've got rocks outside, so crack, somebody tells me they've got rocks, I'm going to let them in, I don't care if it's ten pounds worth of crack or a thousand pounds, I'm going to let that person in because I'm an addict." He didn't see it as a way of you know, kind of saying "I'm not responsible" or something. He was just being genuine. It was genuinely that's what happens, it was a very functional answer.
>
> (Glen, outreach worker)

Compounding this, the apparent initial complicity from people to allow others into their home when faced with withdrawal and the desire to maintain regular use of these drugs can also mean that they are not always provided with suitable 'victim' status in such 'quasi-cuckooing' cases. The various social, legal and cultural contexts required for victimhood to be recognised do not materialise (see Walklate 2007). Instead, when faced with these scenarios, the police and other agencies can sometimes pursue punitive responses. As one drug service worker outlined:

> There's this big cohort of organisations, police, the council, that go, "oh, that person hasn't been properly cuckooed, they let them in." But it's never that straightforward, you know? Have you ever rattled? Have you ever clucked? Because if you haven't you don't know the pressure that person is then under. The physical and emotional pressure to use or to, you know? That's something you don't measure in a numerical scale, because it's emotional. And it's physical and it's there. You know? Actually if somebody then rocks up and says, "Yes, I'll sort you out, mate. I'll square that out for you. Have you got somewhere we can go and use? Have you got somewhere we can go and stay?" What's that person likely to do in that state? Say no? And then they're in the door. They're there. They've taken it over.
>
> (Alex, drug service worker)

This punitive response to 'quasi-cuckooing' cases by the police and others is arguably problematic in and of itself, especially when considering the frequently voiced policing aims of recognising and responding to vulnerability (College of Policing 2023). Its capacity to generate further challenges by making engagement with drug treatment services for the affected person even more difficult demonstrates how the drug policy environment to reproduce itself when enacted upon by relevant practitioners. Far from reducing drug-related harms, the features of this particular policy environment, built on political-economic choices and moral positions, appear to often have the capacity to produce cuckooing.

Conclusion

Based on the conceptualisation of cuckooing as a drug market-related harm (i.e. 'home takeover' scenarios typically involving people who use drugs being exploited by people involved in drug supply), the drug policy environment represents a core aspect of the cuckooing risk environment. Drug policy is a complex, contested and controversial area, with nuanced and accurate discussion regularly buried beneath overly simplistic and bold claims (Ritter 2022). Yet it is a vital area to interrogate to fully understand cuckooing. Covering three core aspects of this policy domain, this chapter has considered the role of this policy environment in making people structurally vulnerable. For each of these, the role(s) they play has been interpreted broadly, incorporating nuanced aspects informed by the academic literature, while retaining the insights provided by those interviewed who had significant knowledge on cases. Doing so is a way of trying to achieve the difficult task of balancing a suitably sophisticated appreciation of the policy environment with the nature of the insights and experiences of those who experience the effects of the policies themselves.

One of the most important insights in this chapter is how the powerful forces associated with the drug policy environment structure the actions of the various actors involved in cuckooing. One group of actors is those explicitly involved in cuckooing scenarios themselves. Building on threads raised in previous chapters regarding the constrained agency of those affected, analysing the drug policy environment provides further insight into why people make choices and undertake actions that seemingly make themselves more at risk. Another group of actors whose actions are structured by the drug policy environment is those who are involved in the responses to cuckooing. Police officers who implement and enforce prohibitionist drug policies can generate cuckooing-related harm in various ways by (re)producing and exacerbating features of the risk environment. It is vital that the role of these 'street level bureaucrats' (Lipsky 1980) within this policy environment is recognised while connecting this to the political choices that create the policy environment. Such analysis builds on the legacy of risk environment studies that have highlighted the negative consequences of social control measures relating to drugs, as well as the small body of work that has specifically raised this in relation to cuckooing (Coomber et al. 2023; Moyle 2019; Spicer 2021). For direct, practical considerations, such critical reflection of police action, combined with the recognition of the reflexivity of some officers working in this area, points towards suggesting what an enabling environment might look like.

References

Bacon, M. (2016) *Taking Care of Business: Police Detectives, Drug Law Enforcement and Proactive Investigation*. Oxford: Oxford University Press.

Bacon, M. and Seddon, T. (2020) Controlling drug users: Forms of power and behavioural regulation in drug treatment services. *The British Journal of Criminology*. 60 (2), pp. 403–421.

Black, C. (2021) *Review of Drugs: Phase Two Report*. London: Home Office.

Coliandris, G. (2015) County lines and wicked problems: Exploring the need for improved policing approaches to vulnerability and early intervention. *Australasian Policing: A Journal of Professional Practice and Research*. 7 (2), pp. 25–36.

College of Policing (2023) *Recognising and Responding to Vulnerability-Related Risks*. London: College of Policing.

Coomber, R., Bacon, M., Spicer, J. and Moyle, L. (2023) Symbolic drugs policing: Conceptual development and harm reduction opportunities. In: M. Bacon and J. Spicer (eds). *Drug Law Enforcement, Policing and Harm Reduction: Ending the Stalemate*. London: Routledge, pp. 87–110.

Coomber, R. and Moyle, L. (2018) The changing shape of street-level heroin and crack supply in England: Commuting, holidaying and cuckooing drug dealers across 'county lines'. *British Journal of Criminology*. 58 (6), pp. 1323–1342.

Eastwood, N., Fox, E. and Rosmarin, A. (2016) *A Quiet Revolution: Drug Decriminalisation Across the Globe*. London: Release.

Goldstein, P. (1985) The drugs/violence nexus: A tripartite conceptual framework. *Journal of Drug Issues*. 15 (4), pp. 493–506.

Harding, S. (2020) *County Lines: Exploitation and Drug Dealing among Urban Street Gangs*. Bristol: Policy Press.

Harris, J. and McElrath, K. (2012) Methadone as social control: Institutionalized stigma and the prospect of recovery. *Qualitative Health Research*. 22 (6), pp. 810–824.

Jacques, S. and Allen, A. (2015) Drug market violence: Virtual anarchy, police pressure, predation, and retaliation. *Criminal Justice Review*. 40 (1), pp. 87–99.

Keay, S. and Kirby, S. (2018) Defining vulnerability: From the conceptual to the operational. *Policing: A Journal of Policy and Practice*. 12 (4), pp. 428–438.

Lipsky, M. (1980) *Street-Level Bureaucracy: Dilemmas of the Individual in Public Services*. New York: Russell Sage Foundation.

MacCoun, R. and Reuter, P. (2001) *Drug War Heresies: Learning from Other Vices, Times, and Places*. Cambridge: Cambridge University Press.

Macdonald, S. J., Donovan, C., Clayton, J. and Husband, M. (2022) Becoming cuckooed: Conceptualising the relationship between disability, home takeovers and criminal exploitation. *Disability & Society*. DOI: https://doi.org/10.1080/09687599.2022.2071680

Moore, D. and Dietze, P. (2005) Enabling environments and the reduction of drug-related harm: Re-framing Australian policy and practice. *Drug and Alcohol Review*. 24 (3), pp. 275–284.

Moyle, L. (2019) Situating vulnerability and exploitation in street-level drug markets: Cuckooing, commuting, and the 'county lines' drug supply model. *Journal of Drug Issues*. 49 (4), pp. 739–755.

Rhodes, T. (2002) The 'risk environment': A framework for understanding and reducing drug-related harm. *International Journal of Drug Policy*. 13 (2), pp. 85–94.

Ritter, A. (2022) *Drug Policy*. London: Routledge.

Robinson, G., McLean, R. and Densley, J. (2019) Working county lines: Child criminal exploitation and illicit drug dealing in Glasgow and Merseyside. *International Journal of Offender Therapy and Comparative Criminology*. 63 (5), pp. 694–711.

Seddon, T. (2020a) Markets, regulation and drug law reform: Towards a constitutive approach. *Social & Legal Studies*. 29 (3), pp. 313–333.

Seddon, T. (2020b) Immoral in principle, unworkable in practice: Cannabis law reform, the Beatles and the Wootton report. *The British Journal of Criminology*. 60 (6), pp. 1567–1584.

Spicer, J. (2021) *Policing County Lines*. London: Palgrave.

Spicer, J., Moyle, L., & Coomber, R. (2020) The variable and evolving nature of 'cuckooing' as a form of criminal exploitation in street level drug markets. *Trends in Organized Crime*. 23 (4), pp. 301–323.

Stevens, A. (2017) Principles, pragmatism and prohibition: Explaining continuity and change in British drug policy. In A. Liebling, S. Maruna and L. McAra (eds). *Oxford Handbook of Criminology*. Oxford: Oxford University Press, pp. 825–845.

Stevens, A. (2022) New prospects for harm reduction in the UK? A commentary on harm reduction and the new UK drug strategy. *International Journal of Drug Policy*. DOI: https://doi.org/10.1016/j.drugpo.2022.103844

Stevens, A. (2024) *Drug Policy Constellations: The Role of Power and Morality in the Making of Drug Policy in the UK*. Bristol: Policy Press.

Stevens, A., Hughes, C. E., Hulme, S. and Cassidy, R. (2022) Depenalization, diversion and decriminalization: A realist review and programme theory of alternatives to criminalization for simple drug possession. *European Journal of Criminology*. 19 (1), pp. 29–54.

Transform (2009) *After the War on Drugs: Blueprint for Regulation*. Bristol: Transform.

Wakeman, S. (2014) 'No one wins. One side just loses more slowly': The wire and drug policy. *Theoretical Criminology*. 18 (2), pp. 224–240.

Walklate, S. (2007) *Imagining the Victim of Crime*. London: McGraw-Hill.

Winstock, A., Eastwood, N. and Stevens, A. (2021) Another drug strategy for the UK. *BMJ*. DOI: https://doi.org/10.1136/bmj.n3097

Woods, N. (2016) *Good Cop Bad War*. London: Ebury Press.

5 Policing the cuckooing risk environment

Cuckooing cases regularly come to the police's attention and fall under their remit, meaning officers are often deeply involved in responding to them. This is heavily influenced by the policy environment that they operate in and reproduce. Perhaps the most relevant aspect of this is the typical actors who are involved in cuckooing (e.g. people who use drugs and people involved in drug supply), as well as how it connects to specific crimes (e.g. violence and exploitation), more general crime trends (e.g. County Lines drug supply) and policy agendas (e.g. vulnerability). This is not to say that the police have a footprint on every cuckooing case that occurs. Among other things, its clandestine nature within the subterranean drug market milieu means they will often be unaware of many incidences. On a practical level, though, the police can be seen as the main operational drivers in the response to cuckooing (Spicer 2021a). They have also been fundamental to the very notion of what cuckooing is and how it is understood. As set out in the opening chapter of this book, when tracing the process that has occurred over the past decade of cuckooing being formally identified, framed as a distinct 'problem' and placed onto the policy and practice landscape, it has been the police that have arguably been central to setting this agenda. Nationally and locally, this has resulted in the police being a dominant voice in the discursive framing of the problem of cuckooing and leading the response to it (see Harding 2020; Macdonald et al. 2022; Spicer 2021b for further insights into the ramifications of this).

For better or worse, the police therefore play a central role within the cuckooing risk environment. As an organisation with unique powers and symbolic qualities (Loader 1997) they shape the nature of this environment and its features. The day-to-day work of individual police officers, who engage with cases and the range of stakeholders involved, means they simultaneously interact with and (re)produce this environment through their actions. Taking this as its starting point, this chapter focuses specifically on the role of the police within the cuckooing risk environment. Many studies have highlighted the role of policing in producing drug-related harms (Burris et al. 2004). This chapter takes inspiration from this body of work and attempts to build on

DOI: 10.4324/9781032705569-5

its legacy of important critical insights. However, by deploying the notion of 'harm reduction policing' (Bacon and Spicer 2023), it also recognises the unique position the police have in relation to responding to cuckooing as a drug market-related harm and considers the potential capacity for them to play a more positive and progressive role in reducing the harms of cuckooing. To do so, the perspectives on the policing of the cuckooing risk environment from two groups are analysed. First, the experiences of practitioners who have worked with the police in relation to cuckooing are considered. Second, the perspectives of the police themselves are given due consideration, with this providing important insight into how and why certain actions are undertaken. Finally, the chapter critically considers the role and influence of 'County Lines' being placed on the policy agenda and the contradictions generated by the policing of this area. Doing so provides a unique analysis into this aspect of the cuckooing risk environment and its implications.

Playing second fiddle: working with the police

While the police are typically (self)positioned as the lead organisation in the response to cuckooing, for other practitioners, this dominance sometimes raised significant challenges when working on cases. The range of practitioners interviewed generally had a strong desire to work in partnership with the police and engage in multi-agency collaboration. This was considered important and mutually beneficial and could lead to achieving some genuine success if undertaken appropriately. Yet the fact that work on cuckooing was typically predicated on the police being the leaders of the responses meant that at times there were perceptions that little support was being explicitly given to others working in this area. Rather than being recognised as knowledgeable, well-positioned practitioners with the capacity to undertake meaningful work in the response to and prevention of cuckooing, their capacity to bring particular professional experience and expertise was felt to sometimes be overlooked. Instead, the responses to cuckooing, shaped by the policy environment, were considered to be unevenly orientated around supporting the activities and desires of the police.

An example of this was discussed by a housing officer who focused on the content of the most recent government drug strategy entitled *From Harm to Hope* (HM Government 2021). She was frustrated by the lack of explicit attention given to cuckooing within this influential drug policy document. Regarding the minimal attention it did receive, she viewed the general promotion of 'multi-agency work' as vague and broadly insufficient for helping them attempt to reduce this harm and undertake what was often considerable work in this area. As she discussed:

> Even that latest Drug Strategy, did you word search it for cuckooing, Jack? One word for 'cuckooing' I think I found in it out of the whole thing.

> And basically it was like "Oh we are just going to get all agencies to work together to resolve cuckooing." But actually it's like there's nothing there to support us to do that at all and that's a big part of the problem as well, there's nothing there really that's going to help us.
>
> (Emily, housing officer)

These feelings and the general challenges associated with collaboration were often amplified by some of the actions taken by the police in relation to specific cases of cuckooing. Police responses against some of the people that other professionals worked with sometimes led to frustration and confusion. Stressing the messy, complex nature of 'quasi-cuckooing' (Spicer et al. 2020), the decisions to take punitive action against occupants in some cases that did not present as classic 'parasitic' forms of exploitation were interpreted as evidence that some local police officers seemingly failed to appreciate the complexities of cuckooing or had the desire to do so. This contrasted with the general policy shift and discursive framing aligned with the 'vulnerability zeitgeist' (Brown 2014) that encourages exploitation to be suitably recognised and responded to appropriately. While this vulnerability agenda has been promoted nationally as a macro-level feature of the policy environment, it has also trickled down to the micro level and is regularly voiced in local meetings. A consequence was that for those practitioners who were working with and supporting these people, stated desires by their local police to appropriately recognise 'vulnerability' and orientate their response accordingly could sometimes ring hollow if the actions they took in the context of some cases seemingly contradicted this. One interviewee outlined their frustrations when reaching out to a local police officer about someone she worked with being affected by cuckooing:

> I tried to contact the new beat manager to have a bit of a conversation around that and like to keep an eye on this individual and whatnot and he was just like, "is your client pressing charges? No? Yeah, can't do anything then, bye." So that is extremely difficult because for me personally. I'm a social worker by trade so, I always have an eye on like kind of stigma, prejudice. I know my clientele, I have been working for over eight years with people with a background of homelessness, drug use, street sex work, prison history, all the good stuff, you know. And I know that the kind of stigma that is applied to my particular client group is huge, I understand that. But I also firmly believe that the role of law enforcement is not to be selective about who they would like to protect. That also includes homeless people and people with drug use issues, right. So that is a major kind of road block right there. It's like talking to a wall essentially, with that officer, it's like, he's absolutely unresponsive, doesn't appear to really care.
>
> (Pam, outreach worker)

Based on these experiences and perceptions, at times such apparent contradictions could seemingly also make those working in other organisations wary of sharing too much with the police out of fear that it could lead to negative repercussions for the people they worked with. This almost inevitably weakened the principle of a collaborative, 'joined up' approach that is often promoted in policy guidance. Speaking about this, a housing officer outlined such experiences and associated concerns:

> I think they often just view it as antisocial behaviour. A lot of our clients will say things like "oh I'm alright with them being here" initially, so it almost looks like they've been invited in. Sometimes they probably have been invited in initially but then that relationship changes once they are in and I think trying to get that over to the police and other agencies about "yes actually they did invite them into the property" is tough. That thing of, they thought they were their friends but this is what's happening now and this person is scared and they are starting to realise that they can't access parts of their own property and there's things going on in the property that they don't agree with. It is difficult to share that with them sometimes and getting them to understand that.
>
> (Ben, housing officer)

The complexities of 'quasi-cuckooing' and the responses to it are again visible here. For many workers in partner organisations, such cases are seemingly interpreted first and foremost as incidences of cuckooing. This is not to say that they are blind to the complexities of such cases or that those affected might have acted in ways that do not conform to 'ideal' victims (Christie 1986). Yet the power differential, exploitation and nature of the situation are recognised as being one that justifies viewing it as 'cuckooing' and being responded to accordingly. In comparison, some police officers exposed to similar cases can differ in their interpretations. This is not to suggest that they may not recognise power imbalances or the presence of coercion, force or even exploitation. But the complex nature of the scenario and the apparent initial willingness of the occupant to allow access to their home mean that it can be interpreted in a different way and lead to more criminal justice-orientated police actions.

Of course, because of their societal role, powers and typically being the lead agency on cuckooing cases, the police's interventions are typically often the most significant. The outcomes of these therefore seemingly explain how this mismatch of interpretation about such cases and what the appropriate responses should be leads to reservations about other workers fully engaging with the police in future cases. This appears problematic on multiple levels. For effective partnership work to take place, communication and information sharing based on levels of trust need to occur. It also runs the risk that for more clear-cut 'parasitic' cuckooing cases where the police are likely to be willing to treat those affected as purely vulnerable victims, information may not be shared with them for fear about negative outcomes.

Culture, partnership work and the vulnerability agenda

Underpinning many of the practitioner's experiences of working with the police on cuckooing cases were more general reservations and frustrations relating to features of police culture. Several interviewees spoke of a barrier they felt existed between them and the police, with this often appearing to be fundamentally cultural in nature. Inevitably such cultural differences touched on a range of issues, but specifically important were those that related to how the challenges and complexities of the lives of people who are cuckooed were interpreted by police officers. One outreach worker, for example, recounted his experience of providing training on trauma-informed practice to local police officers and how it was received:

> I really do think there's something there about training for those coppers though. So, we did actually try this in my previous role. We did try to do some trauma training with a few of the local police officers. And they came along and they did sit through it and they did listen. And you think beforehand, well hopefully this can help, you know, help them see things and understand things. But I realised that it probably didn't go massively well when I think I heard one of the guys refer to it as "fluffy bollocks" afterwards. I don't know if he intended me to hear it or not. He might have he might not, but yeah that wasn't so great.
>
> (Glen, outreach worker)

Those familiar with the literature on police occupational culture are unlikely to find such experiences overly surprising (see Reiner 2010). While police culture is not static or homogenous, even within the contemporary context where notions of 'vulnerability' have come to the fore and concerns around taking issues such as 'trauma' more seriously are promoted, familiar features of 'cop culture' appear to endure (Bacon 2022; Loftus 2010). For those working in partner agencies and exposed to this culture, such experiences could be highly significant. They left a lasting impression about occupational cultural differences, sending 'signals' about what police work is, who police officers are and what should be expected of them (Innes 2014). Most importantly, this seemingly had the capacity to both consciously and unconsciously feed into how they decided to engage with the police on the issue of cuckooing.

The existence of different occupational cultures between the police and the various other organisations they encounter or work alongside has been identified consistently in various contexts (McCarthy and O'Neill 2014). Based on the commonly identified features of these cultures, it is perhaps unsurprising that complex and messy notions of concepts such as 'vulnerability', 'exploitation' and what it means to be a victim of cuckooing might sit more easily with those working in other organisations, compared to the more 'black and white' world outlook and cultural dispositions classically associated with those working within the police (Reiner 2010). Yet, while non-police interviewees suggested that the impact of the 'vulnerability zeitgeist' in the areas of cuckooing and elsewhere had generally been a positive move that they were in favour of, there were also some intriguing critical reflections about how closely its discursive framing fitted with the 'grey area' realities of cuckooing.

A drug service manager, for example, positioned the vulnerability agenda in opposition to a 'law and order' approach. Discourses of vulnerability, he suggested, were sometimes overly simplistic and unrealistic to the messy realities of what actually took place in many cases of cuckooing. Yet, while not losing sight of its potential limitations, aligning their practice with the features of this contemporary policy environment allowed them to pursue the types of approaches to their work that they sought and promote them to others. Most notably in the context of partnership working in cuckooing cases, it was suggested as providing a potential cultural bridge for engaging effectively with the police:

> There are conversations happening out there. County Lines and cuckooing are getting discussed by the police a lot. And they're discussing it with us, And I think they are being discussed in a healthier way than I've seen before, where it's not just about drug dealers, bad people open their doors to drug dealers – bad, let's shut these houses down. But actually there's an acknowledgement that there are needs and vulnerabilities of people whose houses have been taken over. I mean in some ways that also makes it a bit too black and white. You know, it's just the opposite. Now it's poor people getting exploited and having their houses taken over by drug dealers. And it's not that simplistic either. But it's nice to be having a narrative of people being exploited rather than nasty drug users, so I think that is a is a positive.
>
> You know, it's funny, I've used that word vulnerability countless times already in this interview haven't I? And it annoys me because it is infantilizing. It's very patronizing. But when discourse isn't nuanced and it is black or white, having an infantilized narrative around vulnerabilities for me is preferable – if we're going to rate these things – to this sort of very negative self-inflicted harm, morally bad drug users who is morally weak, you know. You can work more with it. At least we're looking at people from a needs led perspective rather than a moral war or purely enforcement led perspective. So yeah, it's a tough one, because the truth is actually somewhere in the middle and it's a more of a spectrum and these things are very complex and everyone is different. But sometimes you need to have a strong narrative to pin things on and vulnerabilities is preferable to other things.
>
> (Seth, drug service manager)

Among other things, such reflections demonstrate the capacity of the policy environment not just to feed directly into the activities of those working on the ground but for it to be reflexively navigated in pursuit of preferable forms of action and outcomes. Rather than simply being acted upon, policy shifts are interpreted and given meaning by 'street level bureaucrats' (Lipsky 1980). For cuckooing, an important outcome of this reflexive practice can mean that the work of police officers can be understood and interpreted by others within the context of the policy environment. As already discussed in this chapter, this can have significant implications for how they do (or do not) collaborate with them in the future. But as alluded to in the interview quote by the drug service manager provided earlier, it can also mean that compromises can be made and opportunities developed for fruitful, progressive collaboration. People working in different organisations can draw on the resources available to them within the policy environment to both make sense of their work and influence how they undertake it. Just as the practice of becoming cuckooed itself can be usefully understood as a process of structuration (Giddens 1984), arguably so too can the responses to it. Put simply, the various professionals operating within this policy context draw on the structural resources around them to inform their practice in particular ways, with their actions serving to shape and reproduce it.

When it comes to resources within the policy environment, identifying how formal policy guidelines, agendas and resources can be drawn upon beneficially provides an indication of what an 'enabling environment' for a harm reduction approach to cuckooing might look like. Alongside this, it appears important to remain aware of the important benefits of more 'informal' ways of working and associated means of engaging with people either affected or considered at risk. One outreach worker suggested seeking out a 'sweet spot' somewhere in the middle of these two approaches:

> So, well, I think basically it's about a mixture of formal and informal stuff. And I suppose the reason I'm saying this is because sometimes the informal stuff is quite harder to capture on the risk assessment. But when it comes down to it that stuff you get told can be priceless, the stuff that really matters.
>
> (Glen, outreach worker)

Such insights recognise how those working in areas such as drug treatment, housing and outreach are often well placed to generate engagement with those most likely to experience cuckooing. Various examples were given of positive experiences engaging with relevant people, providing valuable insight into the nature of a potential enabling environment for cuckooing harm reduction. By generating effective engagement through navigating the policy environment and being attuned to the lives of those potentially affected, practitioners were able to promote actions and strategies firmly within the spirit of harm reduction that were grounded in the realities of these people's lives. The insight and relationships that they built with some of the people they worked with meant that more open, honest and realistic discussions could take place:

> So, in the past we've had really practical conversations. It's interesting, I wouldn't maybe do this if I was a landlord, definitely wouldn't do it if I was a copper, but because I've also worked in drug treatment it's meant that we've had really practical conversations. Stuff like, you know, Where do you score? Who do you score with? Like, are you going to go away? Are you going to score somewhere else? Place the problem to another flat? But also really down to earth conversations with people about how your day looks like, if you're going to come back here and use, who're you going to come back with? Because, you know it's difficult, it's trying to get a sense of what the client's life really looks like and then you're having like a really down to earth conversation around how they might manage things. Again, sometimes I write stuff down on a bit of paper and I've thought that looks a bit yes, a bit, you know a little bit dodgy. But you have to, you have to work with the practicalities of people's lives, you can't just say don't let anyone in, stop taking drugs, you know. You need to think at a more granular level, what does life actually look like for that person?
>
> I think there's some mileage in that but it becomes, . . . well if you were trying to write this out as a formal process it becomes a harder thing to see on paper. And I can see from outside my sector, people might, people might struggle to see that written down as well. I mean, I think that's what people have to understand. The reason I'm saying this is there's something about when you're trying to get the community message around about saying that actually these people are just going to keep using [drugs] and we're trying to keep you and them and everybody as safe as possible. But they're not just going to stop practically.
>
> (Glen, outreach worker)

The very nature of such 'practical conversations' opens space for practical, harm reduction-informed measures and an environment that enables such interventions. As demonstrated in the previous quote, those who occupy a different professional position within the policy environment to the police can pursue alternative actions more aligned with harm reduction (see also Richert et al. 2023). Such workers are still influenced and constrained by this environment, with formal structures, guidelines and policies providing a relatively rigid framework to work within. Yet they are also able to work within them in ways that allow them to attend to the complex realities of the lives of the people they work with. Rather than taking their lead purely from ideas dominant in the policy environment that dictate how cuckooing should be understood and what is appropriate as a response, they can engage with the reality of drug use and people's wider lives. This allows them to not just listen to the answers they receive but respond to and act on them in ways not available or tolerable to police officers.

Drugs policing, cuckooing and harm reduction

So far, this chapter has focused on the experiences of practitioners when working with the police or becoming exposed to their responses to cuckooing. While it's important not to fall into the trap of presenting police actions simplistically or as overly homogenous, in some cases their responses were seen to represent an unhelpful, punitive approach. A blunt criminal justice orientation led to the harms experienced by those affected sometimes being overlooked or occasionally even made worse. Such responses were also seen to contradict not just the desires of those working in other organisations but also the features of the contemporary policy environment. All of this is vital to recognise. Yet, despite the harms associated with the policing of this area and the capacity for them to be amplified (see Spicer 2021b), there arguably remains capacity for the police to be a force for good, a helpful service for those in need and for them to work more productively in this area (Bacon 2022). At the very least, given that the police will almost inevitably remain the lead organisation responding to cuckooing for the foreseeable future, there is a pragmatic rationale for thinking about the reconfiguration of the policing of this area and how police officers could go about their work differently.

At one level, thinking about the policing of cuckooing and how it could be done differently can be undertaken theoretically. A suitable lens for doing so that complements the risk environment approach is the notion of 'harm reduction policing'. As an increasingly prominent framework and set of guiding principles, this is becoming progressively relevant both within academia and among some of those tasked with the practical undertaking of drug policing itself (Kammersgaard 2019). Elsewhere, Matthew Bacon and I have proposed a definition of harm reduction policing as "*policing measures that aim to reduce the adverse health, social, and economic consequences of drug use, drug markets and the efforts to control them through the criminal justice system*" (Bacon and Spicer 2023, p. 14). Applied in the context of cuckooing, this lens provides useful insights for thinking critically yet practically about how the police should respond to cuckooing in the 'here and now', as well as providing room for thinking about how they could respond to cuckooing in the future. It encourages a wider, more holistic perspective on what policing measures should be pursued, what should be avoided and developing an understanding of what the ramifications of police (in)action might be. Such reconfiguration also stresses the more general limitations of drug policing and helps steer away from blunt, law enforcement approaches that often offer little more than a superficial, symbolic veneer of success (Bacon 2016; Coomber et al. 2023). Almost inevitably, by doing so, some of the features of an 'enabling environment' that prioritises reducing the varied harms of cuckooing can begin to be sketched out.

On its own, however, this theoretical endeavour can only be taken so far. To complement the conceptualisation of policing cuckooing through the framework of 'harm reduction policing' and to make it sufficiently meaningful, it is essential to take note of the empirical realities that underlie current police practice. In particular, it is important to consider how policy trends influencing the broader undertaking of policing may shape how cuckooing is responded to. The police operate in and are influenced by the wider policy environment in which they are situated. As discussed earlier in this chapter, they simultaneously play a role in shaping and reproducing it themselves. Drawing on insights from police officers about their work in this area provides a useful way of understanding both how and why police actions are undertaken.

Structures and actions between policing teams

The interplay between police action, organisational structure and policy environment is visible in how different police teams can interpret cuckooing cases in different ways and have different resources at their disposal to engage with them. Such differences appear to specifically revolve around the contrast between 'response' police teams and 'neighbourhood' police teams. Reductions in police funding during the last decade of austerity were described by officers as having significantly limited the capacity of neighbourhood teams. In the context of cuckooing this was regarded as problematic given that, being grounded in the ethos of 'community policing' (Fielding 1995), these locally orientated teams were arguably the best placed to engage with and respond to such cases. Yet because of the apparent scaling back of neighbourhood policing and associated lack of resources, they had limited capacity to identify incidents of cuckooing and sometimes struggled to cope with providing a suitable level of support for those affected when they did engage with them. As one neighbourhood officer noted:

> I am on the neighbourhood team and to be honest the reality is we haven't really got the staff capacity or the knowledge to target it quickly. So I think it is less than I expected before I started here that we get the information about residents being cuckooed. And actually it is more that we get a feel for it or we hear about it after it's happened – so happening in live time is much less common. And identifying somebody who is potentially being a victim of cuckooing entails a lot more work and we then take responsibility for that person. That's not saying we should turn a blind eye to it but when we decide we are going to identify them as a victim of cuckooing, or, you know, as a vulnerable person that we should be supporting. But it gives us an obligation to treat somebody in a way that we are now saying "well this

> is how someone should be treated". That does give us resources issues, safeguarding issues, because really we just can't always put in place everything that we might want to, or that people might expect us to.
>
> (Jean, police sergeant)

A consequence of neighbourhood police teams not having the resources to become aware of cuckooing cases in their early stages, or necessarily having the capacity to effectively safeguard those affected, was that it was often officers based within the 'response' teams who became exposed to these cases instead. This could lead to actions and outcomes that failed to align with the more nuanced approach favoured by neighbourhood officers that recognised vulnerability, sought to generate rapport with those affected and could be broadly viewed as something moving towards a 'harm reduction' approach to the policing of cuckooing. Part of these response team's actions were attributed to the differences in the day-to-day occupational culture that was ascribed to those officers working within these teams. As the neighbourhood sergeant outlined:

> Response do go in to deal with it but they are just sticking a plaster on it really a lot of the time you know. And those response officers often will just think, you know, "yes they are vulnerable but they don't have to be doing what they are doing". It's a bit of the same as in the olden days when they used to say "well that woman can leave her domestic situation", you know? So you've got to educate officers to understand that that victim is probably quite powerless because of the balance of power in that scenario. You know you've got five men who turn up with knives, you ain't gonna just say "fuck off, just leave my house" are you? No, you are going to do exactly what you have to do to keep yourself alive.
>
> (Jean, police sergeant)

Related to this, part of the discrepant and often problematic ways that response officers engaged with cuckooing compared to neighbourhood officers was due to the different ways they worked and the pressures they faced. Because of the nature of their roles, response officers were described as regularly lurching from one incident to another during their shifts. When exposed to a case of cuckooing as part of this working pattern, this could lead to it either not being appropriately recognised for the exploitative situation it might be or being given superficial treatment. Meaningful safeguarding work combined with a deeper appreciation of the complexities before them was considered something that some response officers were either unwilling or unable to do due to the constraints and pressures they faced as part of their routine work. As another neighbourhood officer went on to explain:

> So Response just won't have time. They don't really do safeguarding, they'll go to the job and do immediate safeguarding. So the immediate

> safeguarding could be to arrest someone or it could be to kick someone out of an address. And then they'll pass it over to us at neighbourhoods to do all the follow up work or the safeguarding unit to do referrals. And they're aware of cuckooing – particularly if they work in [name of area where cuckooing is particularly common]. In fact some of them will be really knowledgeable, they'll get it. But others will not really know or have time. They'll just be like "oh there's a drug user and his mate looks a bit weird. We'll just kick his mate out and that'll be it." And actually, well, when it comes to cuckooing that's not really what it's all about.
>
> (Eve, police officer)

Recognising the apparent differences between policing teams and how different practices are therefore present *within* the police is useful for explaining why certain actions may or may not be taken by certain police officers at certain times. In particular, it sheds light on why there might be inconsistencies in police practice when it comes to cuckooing. It would of course be an overly simplistic and superficial analysis to present this dynamic in a binary sense of community teams representing 'good' policing of cuckooing and neighbourhood representing 'bad'. Among other things, this would overlook the problematic responses and associated outcomes of policing in this area that has occurred more generally (see Spicer 2021b). Yet recognising these differences between teams does point towards why nuance and vulnerability might not always be considered sufficiently deeply or recognised appropriately in some incidences (Bacon 2022).

To return to some of the perspectives of other agencies discussed earlier in this chapter, this may also go some way to explain their confusion and frustration of why police actions did not always align with what their apparent shared aims were and how this may feed into not facilitating collaboration and information sharing. Consider, for example, this quote from an outreach worker regarding their experiences of working with the police on matters relating to cuckooing and the more general vulnerabilities of the people they work with:

> What's happened in the past is we've had specific coppers who are amazing, they might be coppers based on a specific area, with a particular portfolio or something. But then they're rota'd off for a couple of days, two or three days often, and then suddenly it all gets crazy with something kicking off, we need to speak to somebody, and you speak to someone else and they don't know the situation or they might have a slightly different understanding or set of approaches to the situation. So, there's something about you know, 'champions', they'll have a good understanding, always have somebody at the end of the phone, and that's a mixture of slightly high-level stuff but also like the locality kind of

> stuff as well. The challenge for us is that I've often wondered with the police about whether we should go into them in advance and speak to someone and say "look, we're housing this person in your area and I wanted you to be aware that they are vulnerable but they also might create some issues". I genuinely haven't done that though. In fact, I absolutely haven't done that at the start, even though maybe I thought it'd be helpful to have someone involved from day one, because I don't know what response I will get.
>
> I mean, mostly coppers will know through our clients that, the most vulnerable people are also frequent perpetrators in crime. But if I could go with some confidence in advance and say look, can we have a chat about how this, like just to raise this and have a chat about how we might get together going forward, that would, that would be part of my you know, risk management process before we get to the incident. I'm uncomfortable doing that because I don't know what the response would be because I don't think it would be consistent.
>
> (Liam, outreach worker)

Viewed through the lens of harm reduction policing, engaging with neighbourhood policing in the desired way described by this outreach worker would likely be beneficial. Genuine collaboration with open communication and appropriate information sharing would represent an opportunity for preventative work to be implemented more consistently. Appropriate support could be put in place for affected people, with a more nuanced understanding of the elevated risks to being cuckooed that certain people may face. A deeper appreciation of the complexities of cuckooing situations and better chance at early intervention could also provide police officers with a greater appreciation of the situations they become exposed to and promote more effective responses. At the very least it could contribute towards discouraging unhelpful or counterproductive actions if instead it made it more likely that neighbourhood teams were the ones to engage with cuckooing cases at their earlier stages.

Not only does this point towards a suitable model of how effective multi-agency work in this area could operate but perhaps represent elements of what an enabling environment for harm reduction policing could look like in relation to cuckooing. Unfortunately, the various quotes provided in this chapter suggest that this is often not currently happening. Instead, inconsistencies between police responses and a lack of communication appear to produce an environment where information is not always shared, and productive collaborative relationships with other agencies are not always fulfilled to their potential. The outcomes of this can then seemingly reproduce these challenges, with contradictions and frustrations emanating out of the way that some cuckooing cases are policed, leading to even greater wariness from other agencies of engaging with them.

The contradictions of policing County Lines

A final area of relevance in the context of the police's role in the cuckooing risk environment, which builds thematically on the role of the policy environment in influencing the police responses to it, is the role of the 'County Lines' drug supply phenomenon. As discussed in the opening chapter, the emergence of cuckooing onto the UK policy landscape has coincided with and become explicitly attached to 'County Lines' drug supply (Harding 2020; Moyle 2019; Spicer 2021a). In addition to discursive framings around exploitation and vulnerability, one of the main reasons for this is how cuckooing fits into this drug supply model. Put simply, the practice of cuckooing is widely adopted as a strategy by 'out of town' dealers for establishing a space to base themselves while present in a satellite locale (Coomber and Moyle 2018). Yet, while the emergence of County Lines has led to a drive to recognise the harms of cuckooing and respond to those affected accordingly, certain contradictions in the policing of this area are apparent. Two of these are worth specific consideration and provide further insight into the policing of the cuckooing risk environment.

The first of these contradictions of County Lines policing concerns how various local crackdowns targeted at actors involved in drug supply over recent years appear to have amplified levels of drug market-related violence and exploitation. The unfortunate irony of these outcomes was that such drug law enforcement operations were often framed – at least in part – as being a response to the presence of violence, exploitation and other harmful externalities connected to the local drug markets. Aligning with the dialectical enforcement dynamics discussed by Coomber et al. (2023), highly publicised local drug market crackdowns appeared to accelerate the presence of County Lines dealing in certain areas. By sweeping up the 'low hanging fruit' of local dealers, this generated vacuums often filled by 'out of town' dealers who were more likely to employ cuckooing as a practice. Generated, at least in part, by the nature of the policy environment, these contradictive, paradoxical outcomes of local drug market policing were discussed in detail by several interviewees. One drug service worker, for example, outlined what had changed over recent years in the local heroin and crack cocaine market of the area he worked in, often in response to police crackdowns:

> The real problem with cuckooing, the real kind of sea change in my mind happened when the County Lines philosophy of drug dealing really kicked in round here. Because the fundamental change – well it was a bit bizarre really. We had a really big drugs bust about three or four years ago. One hit had nineteen dealers gone – a lot of them local guys. And one of the clients I was talking to on that day, I said, "are you guys going to be ok? Will you put yourselves at risk because there's no drugs around?" And they went, "what do you mean no drugs? They all got nicked this morning at

> 9 o'clock. The main dealers have people in from outside the area within two hours, set up, ready to roll." And then you suddenly got the wakeup call that, actually, although what we deal with is the street-level user, the street-level dealer, this is a business organisation. So we had these stories coming out from the police and the local news and stuff about this local crew they banged up. But we knew what was actually happening behind the scenes, you know. And the County Lines and the cuckooing and stuff, well here we are, it got worse.
>
> (Simon, drug service worker)

Corresponding with the wealth of literature noting the unintended and often counterproductive consequences of drug market crackdowns, the national policy environment, with its recent orientation around the priority of County Lines, appeared to generate certain types of local drug police action that paradoxically intensified the amount of cuckooing occurring. Understood as 'symbolic' displays intended to send out certain 'signals' (see Coomber et al. 2023), these local police actions appeared to generate and amplify the local conditions that made cuckooing more likely, producing an environment that made people more at risk.

The second contradictory feature of the role of County Lines policing in shaping the cuckooing risk environment related to distinctions between different cases of cuckooing and how they were perceived. Specifically, this revolved around comparisons between the more familiar form of County Lines-related cuckooing cases, where an 'out of town' dealer was involved in taking over someone's home, and the perhaps less recognised 'local' cuckooing cases (Spicer et al. 2020). Several interviewees suggested that while the police had often become increasingly willing and able to recognise the exploitation that people might experience in cuckooing scenarios involving County Lines dealers, this did not always translate in the same way to cases involving exploitative, cuckooing drug dealers who were local to the area. While situations might be similar, with exploitation and other harms apparent in both, some police officers were not seemingly always as ready to bestow victim status on those whose home was being taken over by people local to the area. As one outreach worker discussed:

> They [the police] are good with it sometimes, don't get me wrong. But at other times, because they [the dealers] are not coming down from London or whatever they can be viewed in a different way, which I am not sure is overly helpful if I'm being completely honest. And I think . . . well it's a bit like what we touched on a moment ago with that question on "why they are letting them in?". Now if that's County Lines there is an understanding how they've got in. But when it's somebody local that thought process is just "oh they shouldn't have let them in". And that is again, yes it's just really frustrating.
>
> (Britney, outreach worker)

Influenced by the emergence of the County Lines agenda in the policy environment, there have been welcome police advances made over recent years in recognising (and being prepared to recognise) the often-complex exploitation involved in cases of County Lines-related cuckooing (Coomber and Moyle 2018; Spicer 2021a). However, such progress does not always appear to translate into cases that do not align with the common framings of how cuckooing manifests. In one sense, this stresses the importance of recognising the notion of 'local cuckooing' (Spicer et al. 2020). Despite the wider concept of cuckooing being closely bound up in the notion of County Lines and associated discourses, it is vital to recognise that it can occur outside of this specific drug supply context (MacDonald et al. 2022). In a broader sense, aligning with the general theme running throughout this chapter, it demonstrates the role of the policy environment in structuring interpretations and responses to what is (and is not) deemed to be cuckooing victimisation. While the increasing recognition of vulnerability and exploitation within the County Lines policy environment have opened welcome avenues for approaches more in line with harm reduction, challenges remain for this to translate to cuckooing cases that do not fit within the parameters of this particular drug market context.

Conclusion

This chapter's point of departure was that the police and the diverse set of practices that fall under the banner of 'policing' play a central role in the cuckooing risk environment. Drawing on the perspectives of those working both outside of and within the police, the analysis has served to critically interrogate this role. Consistent with the tenets of the risk environment approach, central to this is identifying how certain policing practices can generate conditions that make people more structurally vulnerable to cuckooing and ultimately play a role in producing it. The paradoxical outcomes of County Lines-related drug market crackdowns are a good example of this, building on a significant body of literature regarding the unintended consequences of drug law enforcement. The way that certain policing teams may not have the capacity or desire to respond to cuckooing cases in the manner that wider policy agendas might encourage demonstrates this further, although it is of note that other policing teams often seemingly recognise this. What this suggests is the importance of developing a nuanced perspective on the role of the police in the cuckooing environment and the complexity involved. Underpinning this is the crucial and multifaceted role of the policy environment in both producing the structural conditions that make cuckooing more or less likely and influencing the actions taken in response to cuckooing.

The interplay between the policing of this area and the role of the policy environment is also demonstrated though the challenges relating to partnership working. Occupational culture 'wars' between the police and others are not new, nor necessarily surprising. Similar issues have been identified in the response to other crime and social problems (McCarthy and O'Neill 2014). But they remain important, especially in the context of the 'vulnerability turn' in social policy and the stated desire to work together more and more effectively (Brown 2014). Finding ways for the police and other organisations not just to 'work' together but to navigate and negotiate the policy environment productively appears important. If such working is not achieved or only engaged with superficially, this can exacerbate the cuckooing risk environment. The police can end up falling back on approaches that do not suitably recognise vulnerability, while other organisations can become reticent to engage with them appropriately or share insights and information that could help safeguarding efforts. A spiral based on poor information sharing and inappropriate actions is likely to occur. But, as indicated by some of the insights provided by the interviewees quoted in this chapter, a practical vision for what the productive policing of this area could look like is possible to generate. Built on the theoretical notion of 'harm reduction policing', this points towards what an 'enabling environment' might look like, with the capacity for professionals both inside and outside the police to navigate the policy environment reflexively and find ways to negotiate with it to enable ways of responding to cuckooing that can consistently reduce the harms of cuckooing. Finding ways that the police can support such working – or at the very least not undermine it – represents a central concern for reducing the harms of cuckooing.

References

Bacon, M. (2016) *Taking Care of Business: Police Detectives, Drug Law Enforcement and Proactive Investigation*. Oxford: Oxford University Press.

Bacon, M. (2022) Desistance from criminalisation: Police culture and new directions in drugs policing. *Policing and Society*. 32 (4), pp. 522–539.

Bacon, M. and Spicer, J. (2023) Harm reduction policing: Conceptualisation and implementation. In: M. Bacon and J. Spicer (eds). *Drug Law Enforcement, Policing and Harm Reduction: Ending the Stalemate*. London: Routledge, pp. 13–38.

Brown, K. (2014) Questioning the vulnerability zeitgeist: Care and control practices with 'vulnerable' young people. *Social Policy and Society*. 13 (3), pp. 371–387.

Burris, S., Blankenship, K., Donoghoe, M., Sherman, S., Vernick, J., Case, P., Lazzarini, Z. and Koester, S. (2004) Addressing the "risk environment" for injection drug users: The mysterious case of the missing cop. *The Milbank Quarterly*. 82 (1), pp. 125–156.

Christie, N. (1986) The ideal victim. In: E. Fattah (ed). *From Crime Policy to Victim Policy*. London: Palgrave Macmillan, pp. 17–30.

Coomber, R., Bacon, M., Spicer, J. and Moyle, L. (2023) Symbolic drugs policing: Conceptual development and harm reduction opportunities. In: M. Bacon and J. Spicer (eds). *Drug Law Enforcement, Policing and Harm Reduction: Ending the Stalemate*. London: Routledge, pp. 87–110.

Coomber, R. and Moyle, L. (2018) The changing shape of street-level heroin and crack supply in England: Commuting, holidaying and cuckooing drug dealers across 'county lines'. *British Journal of Criminology*. 58 (6), pp. 1323–1342.

Fielding, N. (1995) *Community Policing*. Oxford: Oxford University Press.

Giddens, A. (1984) *The Constitution of Society*. Cambridge: Polity.

Harding, S. (2020) *County Lines: Exploitation and Drug Dealing among Urban Street Gangs*. Bristol: Policy Press.

HM Government (2021) *From Harm to Hope: A 10-Year Drugs Plan to Cut Crime and Save Lives*. London: HM Government.

Innes, M. (2014) *Signal Crimes: Social Reactions to Crime, Disorder and Control*. Oxford: Oxford University Press.

Kammersgaard, T. (2019) Harm reduction policing: From drug law enforcement to protection. *Contemporary Drug Problems*. 46 (4), pp. 345–362.

Lipsky, M. (1980) *Street-Level Bureaucracy: Dilemmas of the Individual in Public Services*. New York: Russell Sage Foundation.

Loader, I. (1997) Policing and the social: Questions of symbolic power. *British Journal of Sociology*. 48 (1), pp. 1–18.

Loftus, B. (2010) Police occupational culture: Classic themes, altered times. *Policing and Society*. 20 (1), pp. 1–20.

Macdonald, S. J., Donovan, C., Clayton, J. and Husband, M. (2022) Becoming cuckooed: Conceptualising the relationship between disability, home takeovers and criminal exploitation. *Disability & Society*. DOI: https://doi.org/10.1080/09687599.2022.2071680

McCarthy, D. and O'Neill, M. (2014) The police and partnership working: Reflections on recent research. *Policing*. 8 (3), pp. 243–253.

Moyle, L. (2019) Situating vulnerability and exploitation in street-level drug markets: Cuckooing, commuting, and the 'county lines' drug supply model. *Journal of Drug Issues*. 49 (4), pp. 739–755.

Reiner, R. (2010) *The Politics of the Police* (4th edition). Oxford: Oxford University Press.

Richert, T., Stallwitz, A. and Nordgren, J. (2023) Harm reduction social work with people who use drugs: A qualitative interview study with social workers in harm reduction services in Sweden. *Harm Reduction Journal*. DOI: https://doi.org/10.1186/s12954-023-00884-w

Spicer, J. (2021a) *Policing County Lines*. London: Palgrave.

Spicer, J. (2021b) The policing of cuckooing in 'county lines' drug dealing: An ethnographic study of an amplification spiral. *The British Journal of Criminology*. 61 (5), pp. 1390–1406.

Spicer, J., Moyle, L. and Coomber, R. (2020) The variable and evolving nature of 'cuckooing' as a form of criminal exploitation in street level drug markets. *Trends in Organized Crime*. 23 (4), pp. 301–323.

6 The social environment of cuckooing

In Chapter 3, it was suggested that because every case of cuckooing must involve a physical space to be taken over, the role of the physical environment is essential to consider when understanding this exploitative practice. It can also be argued that as cuckooing is an interpersonal act, the social environment is equally essential and demands analytic attention. This final empirically based chapter therefore focuses on the role of the social environment in producing cuckooing, which represents the final type of environment of the wider risk environment framework (Rhodes 2002). This is not to overlook that social factors and sociologically informed arguments have already been given attention in previous chapters. Nor is it to say that other types of environment and associated features will not be referred to at times throughout this chapter. But the fundamental focus of this chapter is on the various features of the social environment and the role they play in producing how and why people become vulnerable to cuckooing.

Conceptualisations of the 'social environment' can often be quite broad, encompassing a range of features. While mindful of the challenges in this, a broad conceptualisation can be of benefit in the type of analysis presented in this book. It is worth remembering that the risk environment approach has been conceived as a "*social science for harm reduction*" (Rhodes 2009, p. 198). Being open to the diversity of the social world therefore promotes adopting a lens wide enough to capture all of the various relevant features in the social lives of the people affected by cuckooing. Accordingly, this chapter considers how the social environment operates at different levels and how these different levels interact. Making connections between macro-social trends and structures, to the intricacies of people's social interactions and relationships, it attempts to provide an account of how cuckooing is both located in and produced by the social environment.

Cuckooing and social exclusion: the dynamics of engagement and trust

To analyse the role of the social environment in cuckooing, it is useful to start at the macro level and consider how this can then relate to, interplay with and inform relevant micro social interactions. The concept of social

DOI: 10.4324/9781032705569-6

exclusion provides a useful analytical tool for this purpose. As a concept it has somewhat fallen out of fashion, at least compared to its popularity during the 1990s and early 2000s, where in the UK, New Labour found it a useful way of suggesting what their policy agenda would address. Following the tradition of 'anomie' in criminology, Jock Young's (1999) influential metaphor of 'social bulimia' rested on the concept as a way of describing the social dynamics of how people become ejected from a late-modern society that has simultaneously culturally absorbed them. Avoiding the trap of using it simply as a synonym for poverty, what Young demonstrated was social exclusion's conceptual capacity to incorporate important aspects such as inequality, polarisation and discrimination, as well as the cultural and emotive responses to these experiences (see also Young 2007). This becomes useful when considering the social exclusion many people affected by cuckooing face, helping to shed light on how they cope with this broader structural marginalisation, the specific experiences of being cuckooed and the dynamics at play between the two.

Combining with other environmental features discussed in previous chapters, many people affected by cuckooing were described as having adverse experiences with what was referred to as "the system". My experiences of visiting many affected people alongside police officers and other workers corresponded with this. The phrase "the system" was notably used by several interviewees to refer to the general structure of society, as well as its various institutions – including the police, social services and the health system. For many of those affected by cuckooing, experiences of exclusion had been a central and consistent feature of their lives. The institutions that represented the state – both literately and metaphorically – had often penalised them, disciplined them, criminalised them or failed to provide the support they desired (see Wacquant 2009). The afflictions of this exclusion, including drug use, unemployment, involvement with the criminal justice system, physical and mental health issues, and unstable housing, had resulted in them being cast to the margins of society (Stevens 2011). Yet, rather than helping, the institutions and the professionals they encountered were often seen to push them even further to the edges. One drug service worker spoke about the social position of the people he worked with who had been cuckooed:

> For most of them, not all, you know, but most, they're not in a good place. And they haven't been in a good place for a long time. And I'm not being a bleeding heart 'whatever' here or anything, I'm not saying they aren't a bit responsible for it a bit, but god, life's tough for them. It's been tough for them for a long time, you know. This world, society, whatever, it's not their friend, it's not set up to make it easier. And they know it, they feel it, they live it.
>
> (Simon, drug service worker)

Arising from experiencing these harsh realities of the 'exclusive society' (Young 1999) were several relevant social dynamics relating to cuckooing. An important one relating to responding successfully to it was how this bred distrust of agencies. For some of those affected, a root cause of why they had ended up experiencing cuckooing was seemingly interpreted as due to the exclusionary treatment by society and its various institutions and organisations. Interpreting organisations and the people working in them as contributors to their marginalised structural position, a threat to the few resources they have, or not providing the support they purported to provide meant they were less willing to engage with them. Despite often having the capacity to help them with cuckooing, it was therefore often difficult to get people who represented 'the system' to be interpreted as being on their side and acting in their favour. As one outreach worker discussed:

> I think it's all about 'the system', going against 'the system'. And the feeling is really that the system is against you. So I do think that is used quite a lot. And it's used within the whole community. It's almost like anything that triggers them, that's the first thing they jump to is 'the system' and that anger to 'the system'. And they back off from anything that might help. And I definitely think with the cuckooing, especially when it's a case of trying to get them out of that situation and back into a better place with their housing situation, that can be tough. And I take the approach of trying to say "We understand. I understand you have been through it. It's all shit. But I will look after you". And that's true, you know, I will. But you can see sometimes they don't buy it.
>
> (Britney, outreach worker)

Similarly, a housing officer discussed how the challenges of engaging with some of the people she worked with who experienced cuckooing were intensified because of the various negative experiences that they had experienced over their lives with formal institutions. For some of those he sought to build relationships with, organisations and the people working for them were often interpreted symbolically as another problem in their lives to be managed or even potential threats to be wary of. This then created barriers for building and maintaining the trust necessary to generate suitable engagement. Speaking about these negative experiences and how interactions between affected people and practitioners were typically structured around negativity and punitive outcomes, he asked:

> And why should they believe that we actually do have their best interests at heart?
>
> (Ben, housing officer)

Reproduced by the dynamics of social exclusion, this trust deficit underpinned many of the challenges in generating engagement.

Another related challenge underpinned by a lack of trust concerned information sharing. Those experiencing cuckooing or being aware of it happening to others in their communities were often wary of providing information about it to practitioners due to the risk of being labelled as a 'grass' and the negative repercussions that could come from being seen to collaborate with the police and others (Rosenfeld et al. 2003). Generating sufficient trust where people were comfortable to volunteer information so that interventions could be implemented was therefore often difficult. This was then sometimes undermined further in some incidences where, having taken the leap of providing information, the subsequent outcomes did not always deliver the positive results that had been promised. In fact, for some, the ramifications could put them in a worse position. One outreach worker outlined such experiences:

> And we've had that conversation and they have finally trusted us and given us information that we can pass to the police. And then they watched everything just get worse than what the client has had to go through. Our client will have had a moment where they get so scared and battered by what's happening – when I say battered with cuckooing it can be physical, or just mentally battered with the fear of what's happening at home as well – that they will come to us. And we are trying to build this big relationship that, you know, this isn't to punish them, this is to help them. But when they do it nothing happens. Or it does happen, but it is like just one arrest, force them out of the house, one arrest and then they let them go and then they are straight back in. And then they get a beating because even if the client hasn't been the person to do that, the client will be the one that's blamed and they know that. So the system then lets them down in that way, you know.
>
> (Britney, outreach worker)

Experiences like these inevitably damage trust, making this population less willing to engage and share information in the future. Another experience capable of breeding distrust while also strengthening hostility involved those who ended up vacating their homes and living on the street having been cuckooed. This decision to abandon their home was often because of the risks and harms associated with being cuckooed. The sense of injustice in having to live out on the streets due to someone having exploitatively taken over their home was reported as being strong in and of itself. But this was amplified when those affected faced harassment or penalties for minor offences while 'sleeping rough'. As one interviewee outlined:

> We have three or four clients that, after been cuckooed, for different situations have had to live out on the streets for however long. And they know as well that the whole time that nobody can help. But what doesn't help either is that that client might do something really small and get arrested

> and go to court and get really heavily reprimanded for something small. Or that client who is sleeping rough will be getting "you can't sleep there and you can't sleep there and stop doing this and stop doing that". And they're getting the grief then when they are out of the cuckooing because they are then sleeping out. So while this is happening to them and nothing happens to the perpetrator that can get away with all the dealing. And that is just one more thing that really doesn't help because they see it as "it's okay for some and not for me".
>
> (Pam, outreach worker)

Interpreted as a process of structuration (Giddens 1984), such experiences demonstrate how the features and experiences of social exclusion become reproduced. This occurs through the process of cuckooing itself, while also being bound up in affected people's interpretation of the situation and the responses to it. Faced with the unenviable combination of their structurally marginalised position and experiences of interpersonal exploitation via cuckooing, for many, few credible options to alleviate this situation are available. If putting their trust in a system that is seen to contribute to their exclusion does not provide the beneficial outcomes that have been suggested, then this marginalisation is likely to become further entrenched and engagement with avenues for help in the future become even less likely. In turn, their vulnerability to being cuckooed becomes heightened.

The shame of being cuckooed

The consequences of both being cuckooed and the associated responses can run deep and be highly affective. These can be internalised and acted upon and can serve to reproduce some of the social conditions and structural predicaments that lead to greater vulnerability to cuckooing. A particularly notable emotive state discussed by various interviewees was shame. While having psychoanalytic roots, shame can be understood as a 'social emotion' and should be understood within its social context (Scheff 2000). In the context of cuckooing, shame appears to play an important role in the social environment. This can include structuring the nature of interactions between those exposed to cases in a 'Goffmanesque' sense (Goffman 1959), as well as influencing affected people's conception of self (Petrunik and Shearing 1988).

One way that shame could manifest in the context of cuckooing were situations where people were the recipients of awareness-raising measures, yet still ending up being affected. A common scenario was for people to have been warned about the risks of cuckooing from various professionals, yet ending up being in a position where not only was their home still taken over, but they then encountered those same professionals as part of the response to the situation. The social interactions arising from this could generate a sense of embarrassment and shameful identity, with this projected onto the situation by the various parties involved (Goffman 1963). Simultaneously, this could be bound up in the affected person's own perception of self, being frustrated that they had been naive to the situation or seemingly unable to resist becoming cuckooed.

This dynamic was demonstrated when I accompanied a police officer and housing officer on a welfare check of a man who had recently been cuckooed. Throughout the visit, he continuously referred to himself as having been "*stupid*" and presented this as the reason why his house had been taken over. In one sense this may have been a sincere form of self-appraisal. However, interpreted 'dramaturgically' (Goffman 1959), it was perhaps also an attempt to pre-empt how he believed he was being interpreted by us and to elicit reassurances that he was not, in fact, stupid. Doing so therefore represented a strategy to mitigate a sense of shame.

Other cases demonstrated a similar process, with feelings of apparent 'stupidity' and shame coalescing around people who had experienced cuckooing. As a housing officer discussed:

> I was talking to a client yesterday just in general about cuckooing. He's been using [heroin] for years, he's been around a long time and he was saying "You know, people get invited in because they are going to get drugs and then the problem is they then feel that they are compromised because they've invited the person in in the first place, so it's harder for them to seek help". He was saying there's an element of, you know, almost stupidity around it. Of people feeling stupid that it's happened. "Oh why did I do this? Why did I let this guy in?". You know, and then that can make it very hard for them to come to us and say "look, I am being cuckooed".
>
> (Andy, housing officer)

An outreach worker similarly recounted a case of cuckooing he had worked on and outlined how the person affected had felt shame in various ways. While this case further demonstrated the emotions generated through the experience, it notably illustrated how this was informed by their social environment, while also reproducing it:

> There is a person here who we worked with who had a couple come back to his flat, used drugs and then that seemed like, you know, that was something he'd agreed to do. You know, everyone was on the same level. Within a matter of weeks, he was living just out of his bedroom and people had taken over his living room and his kitchen and he was frightened to come out of the bedroom. And then he was frightened to tell anyone about it. Partly because he thought he'd be in trouble but also because he just felt ashamed. So there's something about, you know, people not wanting to look weak in front of other people and not wanting to look weak in front of

> you know, in front of their support workers. Nobody wants their self-esteem damaged by saying "I've massively cocked up here, come and help me."
>
> (Glen, outreach worker)

The apparent desire among some of those affected by cuckooing to avoid appearing 'weak' appears to be an important feature of the social environment. Goffman (1967) has framed this dynamic in relation to the concept of 'saving face'. The way people seek to present themselves and the situations they find themselves in are ways of achieving this. If these defence mechanisms – perhaps operating in a similar way to 'techniques of neutralisation' (Sykes and Matza 1957) – are successful and they do 'save face' in the context of victimisation, then they can potentially avoid feelings of shame.

One complex case sheds further light on this. It involved a middle-aged man who, shortly after moving into a flat, was cuckooed by a drug supply network operating in the local market. However, he resisted acknowledging the exploitation that, according to the practitioners who worked with him, he was experiencing in his home and became caught up in a drug police operation. As the criminal justice proceedings played out, he resisted downplaying his involvement in the drug supply operation and the idea that he had in some way been victimised. This ended up with him serving a prison sentence. One interviewee who had worked closely with him before and after his time in prison went on to explain further details:

> He bragged about the fact that he was involved in this big drug bust but it very much became clear later on down the line that he was a victim. You know this is someone with serious mental health issues, homeless, just got into his new house, has been targeted by some really high-level drug dealers that are giving him loads of crack and then are employing him as someone that's involved. I don't think for one second he was in that position because he chose to be. I think he was groomed and was a victim but he himself didn't want to see it that way.
>
> And I think it came down to ego, reputation, maybe he didn't want the homeless community to think that he was a victim. Maybe it was a man thing. I mean toxic masculinity. Maybe he didn't want to admit it, you know. He's someone that's quite proud. He can be direct, like if he didn't like you he would tell you. He was quite direct, quite scary, could be quite intimidating but actually is a soft-hearted big friendly giant if he wanted to be. So I think a few different reasons, maybe it is the whole admitting that "I am a victim" publicly. And he was willing to go to prison for it.
>
> And I worked with him later on, like a year after it happened and he had quite a different outlook on it then, one to one. But I think at the time when it was happening he was actively going around bragging about it: "ha ha I'm in the newspaper." Thought it was big and clever. Maybe it is

> because he didn't have a lot of purpose and much else going on in his life so that bit of time in the spotlight might have made him feel superior.
>
> (Marissa, criminal justice officer)

Attempts to 'save face' (Goffman 1967) and to neutralise the social shame of being cuckooed are seemingly identifiable in this case. At a theoretical level, there are perhaps also reasons to interpret it in line with the classic subcultural dynamics associated with 'reaction formation' (Cohen 1955). Located at the margins of mainstream society, this man had experienced a life marked by insecurity, poor mental health, drug use, unstable housing and societal rejection. Representing his relationship with the drug dealers who took over his home as co-conspiratorial could have represented a solution to the social problems he faced in his life, as opposed to the alternative option of acknowledging it as exploitation and therefore a further example of his social marginalisation. Similarly, the apparent bravado regarding his involvement in drug supply and the coverage he received in the local newspaper could have represented an opportunity for status generation within his social environment. By going to prison through the formal criminal justice appraisal of him as an offender, this avoided the shame of being treated not just as a victim but as a 'dupe' who was unable to maintain security of his home. Being aware of his position at the bottom of mainstream society, his resistance to being considered a victim of cuckooing represented a way of avoiding also being positioned at the very bottom of the illicit market hierarchy and therefore being relegated to the depths of both 'social spaces' (Bourdieu 1991). Whatever theoretical interpretation provides the best fit for understanding this specific case, the wider importance of shame, situated within the social context of the subterranean milieu that many people affected by cuckooing are immersed in, appears clear.

Subterranean social capital

One potential consequence of experiencing social exclusion is hostility towards formal societal institutions. Interacting with and compounding this, another consequence is that people can become 'trapped' in subterranean social worlds that run parallel to mainstream society (Densley and Stevens 2015). Being propelled into illicit drug markets and exposed to the actors involved in them is an obvious example of this and highly relevant for those affected by cuckooing. A more general socialisation by being immersed in these social networks in generating collective behaviours and attitudes is also important when analysing the role of the wider social environment. The concept of 'street capital' is relevant to consider in this context. This is proposed as being the "*knowledge, skills and objects that are given value in a street culture*" (Sandberg and Pedersen 2011, p. 33). As this definition suggests, this form of criminological capital is rooted in culture 'from below' (Young 2011).

Alongside this, an appreciation of the role of the social environment in producing cuckooing must also consider the role of social capital. The concept of social capital has a rich and varied legacy, described by Bourdieu and Wacquant (1992, p. 119) as "*the sum of resources, actual or virtual, that accrue to an individual or a group by virtue of possessing a durable network of more or less institutionalized relationships of mutual acquaintance and recognition*". Taken together, these two forms of capital provide a useful conceptual framework for understanding the features of subterranean social networks and the role they play in producing cuckooing.

As previously discussed, there is often reluctance to provide information to professionals about cuckooing or to be seen to be engaging with agencies more broadly. This is particularly the case in relation to the police but is also apparent with other agencies. The reason for this reticence appears partly based on people's own direct personal experiences with these institutions and the people who work for them. Aligning with the notion of 'street capital' (Sandberg and Pederson 2011), as well as ideas prevalent in the wider subcultural tradition (Anderson 1999), hostility towards the police and others is also seemingly generated by wider cultural norms and associated fears of the repercussions of doing so. These repercussions could be immediate and severe, such as violence. They can also be more subtle and insidious, including being ostracised from their social networks or being given a bad reputation (Rosenfeld et al. 2003).

Various interviewees discussed how this social dynamic related to cuckooing. A neighbourhood police officer outlined how some people's fear of being seen to engage with them acted as a barrier against pursuing safeguarding measures for those vulnerable to this form of exploitation:

> I think everybody is scared of being accused of being a grass. And, you know, those barriers where people don't trust the police because they are more scared of the abuse that they will get, that's a really big challenge. How do you earn that trust from people to make them understand we can help make them safe? I think that's probably one of the biggest inhibitors.
>
> (Carl, police sergeant)

Similarly, drawing on insights derived from a cuckooing case she had been involved with, a criminal justice officer discussed the challenges that information sharing had for their agency. This challenge related to specific people they worked with and among the wider local drug-using community that their work exposed them to:

> So one person who I worked with was a female. She was one that had County Lines in her property. She never once described it as cuckooing and it was a really horrible time in her life and she's now moved on to

> different housing and is not using anymore. She's in a much better place. But I think the way she would describe it is definitely not in the words 'cuckooing' and also it's not something she would openly give information about or talk freely about. I mean I'd have to pry it out of her. I think people are really reluctant to grass and snitch. I mean if you tell that someone who has loads of money and links to dangerous people is doing something, committing a crime from your house, that is going to put you at serious risk. I think a lot of people that are involved with cuckooing, it happens because they are vulnerable and they know for a fact that if they grass then they are going to get seriously hurt. So I think that's one of the biggest problem that we face, is that people are afraid to come forward. Most of the time we know about cuckooing because of intel, word on the street, so and so know that they're dealing from that house and we know a vulnerable person lives there.
>
> (Marissa, criminal justice officer)

The relatively small, tight-knit nature of these communities is important in this context. Wakeman (2016) has documented the importance of the close social bonds among networks of people who use heroin within the UK. Meaningful relationships based on forms of mutual support are essential for maintaining their use, addressing the challenges of social exclusion and generally 'getting by' (see also Bourgois and Schonberg 2009). The nature of these social networks seemingly heightens reluctance to engage and share information. There also appeared to be something about the associated social conditions within these communities that meant cuckooing became more likely. Several different mechanisms were identifiable for how this could occur. In one town, for example, a relatively small community of heroin users who experienced sporadic homelessness was described as a core population who regularly experienced cuckooing. The size of this community and the close ties within it seemingly served to produce certain social conditions that made them susceptible. The significant 'bonding social capital' (Putnam 2000) drawn upon by this population as a resource to stay afloat amid their structural marginalisation meant that those who did end up finding housing within these social networks often became quickly known about, the subject of discussion and targeted by others. As one interviewee explained:

> It is such a small place. And amongst the homeless community and that crowd in town everybody knows each other. So if anyone gets a flat, that's it, everybody knows within a day probably. And it can quickly become a problem because that control goes and you have all sorts of people in there.
>
> (Emily, housing officer)

An outreach worker spoke of a similar dynamic and how the situation could creep up on the person affected, often without them realising it because of the nature of their social environment:

> So, to give you an example based on the experiences of some of the people I've worked with, you might go into town, raise a load of money with some other people, you all score together, you've got the flats, you come back and you use in your flat, and you do that a few more times. Those people, you know, there are different levels of kind of power and dynamics and stuff within homes in the community. Everyone on the streets I would argue is vulnerable because it's dangerous and unhealthy, but there are obviously people who are quite dominant characters. So, you might end up inviting someone back and thinking this is kind of an agreed consensual thing but then you just lose control.
>
> (Glen, outreach worker)

In another town where 'local cuckooing' (Spicer et al. 2020) was more prevalent, a slightly different mechanism was observable. Cuckooing was heavily concentrated in a select few deprived areas, where the illicit drug market and associated social networks had a significant presence. The social capital among these communities again appeared to play an important role as to why and how cuckooing occurred. Most of those living in these neighbourhoods were said to know each other well, often having lived among each other for most of their lives. This seemed to make local cuckooing more likely in some cases and meant those doing the cuckooing were often known well by the people whose homes they took over. As one outreach worker recounted:

> Certainly in [name of Town] the drug-related society is actually quite small. Most of the people here are born and bred within the big estates around [name of Town]. They all know each other, they all go back years. And there is that element often with cuckooing of actually, this is their mates to some extent. And you know even [name of local user-dealer who cuckooed many people in the town] after his death you still won't get many of the community to say "actually he was a nasty piece of work".
>
> (Ryan, housing officer)

Being acquainted with the person who had cuckooed them and losing control of their home through a gradual social process muddied the complex waters of these exploitative set-ups and the recognition of victim status of those affected. Adding to this complexity while further demonstrating the importance of social capital within the context of these subterranean worlds was the role played by some in facilitating cuckooing by helping dealers find somewhere to stay. This undertaking was most closely associated with County Lines cases of cuckooing, with 'out-of-town' dealers seeking out potential 'nests' in foreign locales (Coomber and Moyle 2018). Building on observations I had made while analysing police intelligence during previous fieldwork, as well as from Harding (2020), it was reported that County Lines dealers would often draw on these close-knit social networks by tasking their customers with finding a suitable local flat they could use as their base. Situating this practice within the wider social milieu, one housing officer explained:

> Within that community they all know each other so much. Word spreads like wildfire. So I can be told something at work that nobody is meant to know regarding a client and you go out five minutes later and another client's already knowing and they've all got their own variations of that story. And regarding some people who are part of that community, you know, we've had it where they, yeah basically collaborate with dealers to tell them about potential places they could go to. Maybe collaborate isn't the right word, I don't know. But they've told them about so and so, told them where they live and then sure enough they're in their flat. So they're part of it, you know.
>
> (Alyssa, housing officer)

Though an intriguing aspect of drug market activity, given the nature of these social worlds, it is not necessarily surprising that this cuckooing facilitation occurs. Formed amid the fluidity, tension and uncertainty that underpin drug markets, the social relationships among their participants can be superficial, unreliable and exploitative (Bourgois and Schonberg 2009). The important point it demonstrates, however, is that the social relations within these communities shape vulnerability to cuckooing, with people drawing on their social capital as a resource (Field 2016). The close connections between people within these subterranean social spheres provide the knowledge necessary for the facilitation to occur, while the nature of the relationships between people seemingly shows the capacity for people to conspire against one another.

Conspiring to enable cuckooing is problematic. While a strong 'moral economy' is argued to exist among these communities (Wakeman 2016), there seemingly exists significant capacity for immorality by facilitating the exploitation of people who are likely to be highly vulnerable. Yet it should arguably be recognised that this facilitation is often a specific strategy by those undertaking it, representing a solution to problems they face within their structural constraints. Just as people affected by 'quasi-cuckooing' often provide initial access to their home in return for drugs or money, helping dealers identify suitable 'nests' in return for such reimbursement will likely be based on similar motivations. Of course, another motivation may well be self-preservation. Faced with the prospect of dealers seeking somewhere to base themselves, helping to facilitate a cuckooing set-up elsewhere may represent one of the few strategies available to not end up being cuckooed themselves.

Lack of social capital: loneliness and social isolation

The previous section considered how forms of social capital within communities affected by cuckooing, combined with the cultural features of 'street capital', produce conditions conducive to cuckooing. Continuing this theme, it is worth looking at the other side of the coin to consider the role that a lack of social capital can play (see Macdonald et al. 2022). Social capital includes collective, as well as individual dimensions (Nyqvist et al. 2016). For those affected by cuckooing, it is important to recognise that this is often situated alongside and interplays with their wider experience of social exclusion (Harding 2020; Spicer et al. 2020). While being complex and multifaceted, scrutinising the role of a lack of social capital among some of those affected by cuckooing uncovers an important further feature of the risk environment of this drug market harm. These insights are deepened when connected to the attendant by-products of social isolation and loneliness, which relate to people's perceptions of the deficiency in both the quantity and quality of their social relations (Peplau and Perlman 1982).

One case neatly demonstrated the complex role that a lack of social capital can play in relation to cuckooing. I came across it when joining a housing officer and two police officers to visit a middle-aged woman who used heroin, lived alone and had recently been cuckooed by a County Lines network. Her social isolation was considered one of her main vulnerabilities to cuckooing, with both she and the practitioners suggesting it made it difficult for her to keep people involved in the local drug market out of her home. The recent addition of a man staying in her flat was viewed as a potentially valuable protective factor to help prevent it from happening again, framed through the language of routine activities theory as representing a 'capable guardian' (Hollis et al. 2013). On the one hand, his presence represented reassurance. On the other, however, a lack of information about who this man was and his motivations simultaneously actually generated anxiety that it might actually generate further problems. As the housing officer discussed:

> She has this male friend who she says is going to be her comfort and is going to help her to stay on the straight and narrow. You know, he's going to make her feel comfortable. He won't be living with her but he'll be staying with her a few nights a week. Who this male friend is, well . . . I just have his name but she won't tell me his whole name. I just know him as "Mr M", shall we say? And I have my concerns about him. Now, he could genuinely be a comfort blanket and a safety blanket. And a safety person to be around, so that, he gives off different signals to people around her to say, "sorry, go away. This is, you know, this is a safe place now, go away." So I think having somebody around them is highly good for them. That's a reassuring factor. And I think they become stronger. They're weaker as an individual. But not weaker as a person; just weaker because of their

> vulnerabilities, really, and because of their needs. Yes. So I'm hoping that this particular gentleman is of a good mind – you know, has a good intention, shall we say. But it's definitely the case, people are stronger in pairs.
>
> (Alyssa, housing officer)

Various other cases suggested that experiencing social isolation and loneliness was significant for many people affected by cuckooing. In addition to this being a notable feature in their lives, it was considered to contribute significantly to why some became affected. Experiences of what Weiss (1973) would consider as 'social loneliness' appeared particularly relevant in this context. One interviewee situated this in the day-to-day situations many found themselves in:

> We used to see it in supportive housing. You stick people in somewhere and actually they instantly lose the social contact that they had before. So they become very lonely and they don't have a lot to do. None of them work. None of them have a particularly wide social network. Some have family support. So actually you know it's one of the issues we have to deal with. You put someone in a house and they are instantly lonely and don't have anything to do.
>
> (Ryan, Housing Officer)

Such experiences meant that people often ended up being pulled more deeply into the subterranean social worlds and local drug market activity that could lead to them becoming exposed to cuckooing (see Moyle 2019). This could be difficult to avoid. Even for those aware of this risk and attempting to distance themselves from it, the desire for social interaction amid the isolating monotony of their lives meant that they could nevertheless end up getting dragged into this social milieu. As one housing officer discussed:

> We've got a few clients in a similar situation at the moment and they are all saying the same thing: "actually I am trying to stay out of town as much as I can". And that's because they are aware of the influences. But I think on a day-to-day basis it will be you know, getting their script, getting their fix, having a drink in some cases. And then in most cases a good result is that we are sitting at home watching the telly, to be honest. But that's still pretty soul-destroying day in, day out. So they will wander into town and that's when they meet the people. And if they meet someone who's looking for somewhere to stay that's where the risk starts to arise.
>
> (Andy, housing officer)

For some, beyond socialising with certain 'risky' groups, going one step further and allowing people into their home appeared to represent a way of alleviating problems of loneliness, isolation and boredom. The consequences of this could be an exacerbation of these problems and the underlying reasons why they occurred in the first place. One interviewee recounted this in relation to a case they had worked on:

> I think for the person I was working with it was maybe a way of coping with that social isolation, I think. Having that companionship, letting them in, being part of that activity gave him something to do, basically. He would often describe finding it difficult to say no out of boredom, not just as, you know, coercion from others. He'd describe himself kind of staring at four walls, nothing to do. But then obviously like I said earlier the consequences of that were not good. You see what position he ended up in.
>
> (Laurence, social worker)

In addition to the 'social loneliness' attributed to a lack of social capital, Weiss's (1973) conception of 'emotional loneliness' also appeared relevant. For some, experiences of social isolation and loneliness intertwined with failed prior relationships, experiences of grief and a deep sense of loss. The social relations that could be generated by allowing people into their home, even if aware of the risks of doing so, represented a way of coping with the loss of family members in their lives, whether that be through death, abandonment or other means. Speaking about a case of a woman affected by cuckooing whose children had been taken into care, one interviewee noted:

> We think a lot about attachment issues and about how people form relationships. And we deal with a lot of people who are really damaged by their childhoods and subsequent loss. I work with someone who's had three or four kids taken off her. She's had a pretty colourful past and she's had people in her flat. And sometimes one of the things that is interesting, you know, and I think you see it with her, is that there is sometimes a genuine care element. Like people want, people are seeking connection with others. It's: "I'll invite anyone in because I'm just really lonely". You know, living on the street is chaos but it's not boring and if you want company you'll have other people around.
>
> (Liam, outreach worker)

These cases further reveal how cuckooing is a complex social situation, where isolation, loneliness and boredom converge with interactions in 'risky' social networks that are underpinned by social exclusion and illicit drug market activity. Amid this convergence, people's homes become the social spaces where this complexity plays out. Understanding how and why access is initially obtained, homes are taken over and the process of cuckooing unfolds must acknowledge the role of social capital in influencing the complex social realities that shape people's lives.

This also has implications for the nature of the responses to those affected by cuckooing. Consistent with the risk environment approach, acknowledging the complex social nature of cuckooing stresses the importance of avoiding an over-reliance on getting people to be 'rational' and imparting knowledge on them so that they can make the 'right decisions'. The limitations of this were discussed by one outreach worker:

> We put you in a flat and the biggest thing is being lonely. And these are people who are really, really reaching out for connection but really struggle to work out who's got their best interests at heart and how to manage those situations. So, there's that kind of relational stuff about it as well, you know. And you see this in lots of kind of street-based relationships. I'm talking about this because that's what I do. But people would rather have a shit relationship than no relationship at all and for me that's important. I think when I've talked to landlords and occasionally kind of slightly less emotionally intelligent coppers, I don't think they get that. I think sometimes it's just "I'd rather be with someone who's dangerous, you know, might hurt me, might wreck my tenancy, might do all these things. I'd rather be with anyone than no one at all". And I think that's quite an important thing for me to bear in mind. It's not as simple as saying "just don't have that person in". If you're going to take something away from someone, you need to backfill that space as a worker, you need to provide that connection, that company, befriending kind of peer mentoring, community stuff. But at the same time you're doing that, you're also trying to manage and minimise that active addiction as well.
>
> (Glen, outreach worker)

Such reflections are important for understanding the 'victim blaming' capacity of the cuckooing risk environment. They also suggest what form a better response should take. An enabling environment that successfully reduces cuckooing and associated harms must consider the subjective social context, grounded in people's structural position. If not, interventions into the lives of people affected by cuckooing are unlikely to be effective.

Safety and protection

A final area of the social environment that builds on several of the themes already raised in this chapter concerns people's feelings of protection and safety within their domestic environment. Allowing others access to their home appeared to provide some people with feelings of safety that, for various reasons, they may be seeking out. With dependent drug users being a population that experience high levels of victimisation (Stevens et al. 2007), it is perhaps unsurprising that opportunities to secure greater protection might be attractive. This was compounded by a more general sense of marginalisation and experiences of social exclusion (Kammersgaard 2019). The safety of having others around them could represent a solution to this social problem. As one interviewee outlined when discussing why people may allow others into their homes despite being aware of the risks of being cuckooed:

> A lot of the time the reason why is driven by being in that drug world itself and wanting protection. You know having a drug dealer in my house might protect me from the five other drug dealers that I owe £100. Or it might be people might not rob me anymore. It's a sense of "I am going to have protection". And I've seen that with several of the people we work with.
>
> (Alex, drug service worker)

Similar to many of the other potential 'solutions' discussed already in this chapter, in the context of cuckooing, this often had the paradoxical, unintended consequence of making victimisation more likely. Within these communities, some were seen to prey on people's feelings of safety and presented themselves as a way of offering protection as a strategy to obtain access to their homes. Understood as a process of structuration, people's existing fears and anxieties were reproduced when they experienced cuckooing and related exploitation. As one interviewee outlined:

> There's cases of "yes, I'll protect you", you know. "Yes you've got all those people, you don't want to hang about with them. You don't want to. I'll put up here and make sure nothing bad happens to you" and all that. In the meantime they are destroying the flat in their fits of rage and whatever you know. Keeping them away from seeing family members. Not opening the door to us. Stashing drugs in there.
>
> (Ben, housing officer)

Sometimes, this process could be even more insidious. A drug service worker discussed a case involving a man he worked with, where it was suspected that a physical assault had been orchestrated against him by a drug dealer. The dealer had slowly been gaining access to his flat but was seeking to create a stronger foothold. With the man feeling in need of protection following the assault and continued threats, the orchestrator used this to generate greater access to the man's flat. Upon doing so, it was taken over and used by a drug supply network. As the drug service worker discussed:

> To our knowledge, that individual didn't physically attack the householder, but we think other people may have done. We think he may have got people to either assault or intimidate this client, so that he can then go to this client: "Oh, I'm the only person that can protect you" so he stayed. By doing so he's entrenching himself and entrenching himself and entrenching himself. And the individual, because of a combination of mental health,

physical health, and fear – absolutely fear – felt like they had no other choice.

(Simon, drug service worker)

Similar to other features of the social environment discussed in this chapter, these cases demonstrate the unintended consequences of the choices affected people make within their structural constraints, including how risk and vulnerability are reproduced. Already feeling at risk of victimisation, what represents as the available means of protecting themselves can often lead to further risk. By granting people access to their homes, not only can victimisation become more likely, but it can also be brought closer to home.

Conclusion

Focusing on the multifaceted and complex role of the social environment, this chapter has analysed the role that various social features play in producing cuckooing. While being a drug market-related harm, it is arguably also appropriate and useful to understand cuckooing as a 'social harm'. Doing so helps achieve a deeper understanding of why it occurs, avoids simplistic explanations, and points towards how it can be successfully ameliorated. It also recognises that cuckooing interplays and interacts with other social problems. The various experiences of social exclusion are a clear example. Cuckooing can serve to reproduce social exclusion while simultaneously being a problem that is produced by social exclusion and its various maladies itself. This points to cuckooing being the outcome of a social process that plays out at the micro level of social interaction while being influenced by a range of structural forces. Cuckooing is not necessarily therefore something that simply 'happens' or fits neatly into defined temporal sequences. Instead, it often has long, complex social roots based on people's structural position, representing the outcome of equally complex, emotionally charged social interactions between people who are navigating an often harsh social world.

While sites of exchange, drug markets are also inherently social spaces (Dwyer and Moore 2010). This remains particularly so for heroin and crack markets in the UK, where reliance on face-to-face interactions perseveres compared to the shift to digital platforms increasingly used to source other drugs. The people engaged in these drug markets are often bound together socially, sharing a subterranean social space and the types of social experiences consistent with a life on the margins (Wakeman 2016). Those affected by cuckooing often face myriad daily challenges and need to find solutions to problems. As 'risk navigators', social capital plays a crucial role in the decisions they make and the resources available. This is not to suggest that there is a social atmosphere of conviviality. Instead, faced with a range of social problems ranging from isolation, boredom and loneliness to fear, shame and distrust of societal institutions, the solutions that present themselves can end up generating vulnerability to cuckooing. This can reproduce those very social problems. By recognising this social context and its relationship with structural issues, a fuller appreciation of why cuckooing occurs can be generated. In turn, by acknowledging this complex social reality, more effective responses to this problem can be developed.

References

Anderson, E. (1999) *Code of the Street: Decency, Violence, and the Moral Life of the Inner City*. New York: Norton.

Bourdieu, P. (1991) *Language and Symbolic Power*. Harvard: Harvard University Press.

Bourgois, P. and Schonberg, J. (2009) *Righteous Dopefiend*. Berkeley: University of California Press.

Bourdieu, P. and Wacquant, L. (1992) *An Invitation to Reflexive Sociology*. Chicago: University of Chicago press.

Cohen, A. (1955) *Delinquent Boys: The Culture of the Gang*. Chicago: University of Chicago Press.

Coomber, R. and Moyle, L. (2018) The changing shape of street-level heroin and crack supply in England: Commuting, holidaying and cuckooing drug dealers across 'county lines'. *British Journal of Criminology*. 58 (6), pp. 1323–1342.

Densley, J. and Stevens, A. (2015) 'We'll show you gang': The subterranean structuration of gang life in London. *Criminology & Criminal Justice*. 15 (1), pp. 102–120.

Dwyer, R. and Moore, D. (2010) Understanding illicit drug markets in Australia: Notes towards a critical reconceptualization. *The British Journal of Criminology*. 50 (1), pp. 82–101.

Field, J. (2016) *Social Capital*. London: Routledge.

Giddens, A. (1984) *The Constitution of Society*. Cambridge: Polity.

Goffman, E. (1959) *The Presentation of Self in Everyday Life*. Harmondsworth: Penguin.

Goffman, E. (1967) *Interaction Ritual*. Harmondsworth: Penguin.

Goffman, I. (1963) *Stigma: Notes on the Management of Spoiled Identity*. Englewood Cliffs, NJ: Prentice-Hall.

Harding, S. (2020) *County Lines: Exploitation and Drug Dealing among Urban Street Gangs*. Bristol: Policy Press.

Hollis, M. E., Felson, M. and Welsh, B. C. (2013) The capable guardian in routine activities theory: A theoretical and conceptual reappraisal. *Crime Prevention and Community Safety*. 15 (1), pp. 65–79.

Kammersgaard, T. (2019) Harm reduction policing: From drug law enforcement to protection. *Contemporary Drug Problems*. 46 (4), pp. 345–362.

Macdonald, S. J., Donovan, C., Clayton, J. and Husband, M. (2022) Becoming cuckooed: Conceptualising the relationship between disability, home takeovers and criminal exploitation. *Disability & Society*. DOI: https://doi.org/10.1080/09687599.2022.2071680

Moyle, L. (2019) Situating vulnerability and exploitation in street-level drug markets: Cuckooing, commuting, and the 'county lines' drug supply model. *Journal of Drug Issues*. 49 (4), pp. 739–755.

Nyqvist, F., Victor, C. R., Forsman, A. K. and Cattan, M. (2016) The association between social capital and loneliness in different age groups: A population-based study in Western Finland. *BMC Public Health*. 16 (1), pp. 1–8.

Peplau, L. and Perlman, D. (1982) *Loneliness: A Sourcebook of Current Theory, Research and Therapy*. New York: John Wiley & Sons.

Petrunik, M. and Shearing, C. D. (1988) The" I," the" Me," and the" It": Moving beyond the Meadian conception of self. *Canadian Journal of Sociology*. 13 (4), pp. 435–448.

Putnam, R. D. (2000) *Bowling Alone: The Collapse and Revival of American Community*. New York: Simon and Schuster.

Rhodes, T. (2002) The 'risk environment': A framework for understanding and reducing drug-related harm. *International Journal of Drug Policy*. 13 (2), pp. 85–94.

Rhodes, T. (2009) Risk environments and drug harms: A social science for harm reduction approach. *International Journal of Drug Policy*. 20 (3), pp. 193–201.

Rosenfeld, R., Jacobs, B. A. and Wright, R. (2003) Snitching and the code of the street. *British Journal of Criminology*. 43 (2), pp. 291–309.

Sandberg, S. and Pedersen, W. (2011) *Street Capital*. Bristol: Policy Press.

Scheff, T. J. (2000) Shame and the social bond: A sociological theory. *Sociological Theory*. 18 (1), pp. 84–99.

Spicer, J., Moyle, L. and Coomber, R. (2020) The variable and evolving nature of 'cuckooing' as a form of criminal exploitation in street level drug markets. *Trends in Organized Crime*. 23 (4), pp. 301–323.

Stevens, A. (2011) *Drugs, Crime and Public Health: The Political Economy of Drug Policy*. London: Routledge.

Stevens, A., Berto, D., Frick, U., Kerschl, V., McSweeney, T., Schaaf, S. and Werdenich, W. (2007) The victimization of dependent drug users: Findings from a European study. *European Journal of Criminology*. 4 (4), pp. 385–408.

Sykes, G. and Matza, D. (1957) Techniques of neutralization: A theory of delinquency. *American Sociological Review*. 22 (6), pp. 664–670.

Wacquant, L. (2009) *Punishing the Poor: The Neoliberal Government of Social Insecurity*. Durham, NC: Duke University Press.

Wakeman, S. (2016) The moral economy of heroin in 'Austerity Britain'. *Critical Criminology*. 24 (3), pp. 363–377.

Weiss, R. S (1973) *Loneliness: The Experience of Emotional and Social Isolation*. London: MIT Press.

Young, J. (1999) *The Exclusive Society*. London: Sage.

Young, J. (2007) *The Vertigo of Late Modernity*. London: Sage.

Young, J. (2011) *The Criminological Imagination*. Cambridge: Polity Press.

7 Towards an enabling environment for reducing cuckooing

The old saying goes that "an Englishman's home is his castle". For many people in the UK and beyond, their domestic environment falls far short of this idealistic vision. Their home does not represent a place of sanctuary. It is not somewhere they feel safe, secure and can do as they please. Instead, it can be a place of fear, pain and misery. This book has focused on some of the more extreme cases of these experiences. Those affected by cuckooing can lose complete autonomy of their home, while experiencing a range of other harms such as threats and violence in the process. Yet, while cuckooing represents one of the more obvious and acute ways that someone's relationship with their home can be ruptured, those affected are often not respectively visible in their status as victims. Their embroilment in these exploitative domestic scenarios often comes to represent a by-product of their exposure to the illicit drug market and marginalised structural position. Far from encountering 'ideal' victims who engage as desired, the range of practitioners who become aware of and attempt to respond to these cases are typically met with a range of messy, complex situations, filled with ambiguities. Being situated in and interacting with the wider environment, this makes cuckooing a complex problem to understand and a difficult one to resolve.

The argument that I have set out is that the messy, complex reality of cuckooing must be suitably recognised and appreciated. Rather than shying away from this complexity or falling back onto simplistic explanations, this reality should be met head-on by all practitioners and policymakers working in this area. Researchers analysing cuckooing should be wary of simplistic accounts and draw on relevant theoretical tools to continue to deepen understandings. This analysis can then critically feed back into the level of practice to help develop ideas about what can be done to reduce it and its attendant harms. With that in mind, I wish to draw the book to a close by bringing together some of the key insights that have been put forward in previous chapters and considering how they can be situated in a broader context. This includes setting out some key features of the cuckooing risk environment addressed in the previous chapters. It also includes attempting to demonstrate its wider capacity to make disciplinary contributions to criminology and what an enabling environment for reducing the harms of cuckooing might look like.

DOI: 10.4324/9781032705569-7

Indoor drug places: ghosts and homes

Paul Rock's (2005) observations regarding criminology's disciplinary tendency toward 'chronocentrism' appear as relevant now as ever. For various reasons, criminologists continue to lean towards the 'new' and the 'recent' at the expense of giving due consideration to history and precedent. Some of the discourses surrounding County Lines over recent years are a good example of this (Spicer 2021a), and there is a risk of this slipping into analyses of cuckooing too. Hopefully, this book represents a progressive step down a path to move discussions about cuckooing forward into the future. Looking back into the past is useful for making sure this progressive path leads in the right direction.

Situating cuckooing in a broader historical context suggests that it represents a recent addition to a long line of other 'indoor drug places' (Parkin and Coomber 2009). The opium dens of the nineteenth century, for example, famously became attached in the public and literary imagination to Chinese immigrants and some of the murkier areas of the East End of Victorian London (Berridge 1978). Fast forward to the latter half of the twentieth century, and the 'crack house' became emblematic of fears about inner-city crime and violence in the US, with media-stoked fear fuelling the 'War on Drugs'-style police responses (Reinarman and Levine 2004). As another 'indoor drug place', cuckooing similarly relies on particular contemporary contextual features. This includes being primarily associated with a certain type of drug supply in the form of County Lines, as well as a particular conception of those affected in the form of the 'vulnerable' user of heroin and crack. More broadly, it represents a further mechanism for how drug market-related violence 'comes home' (Stitt and Auyero 2018)

Various other examples could be given of indoor drug places that have 'popped up' over time, ranging from so-called 'shooting galleries' (Bourgois 1998) to 'rave warehouses' (Ingham et al. 1999), all the way to the harm reduction intervention of drug consumption rooms. Here is not the place for an exhaustive historical account of all of these. The key point is that in various shapes and forms, cuckooing has some precedent. It has similarities with the numerous other indoor venues that have been understood primarily in terms of the presence of drugs and drug-related actors, while being distinct in and of itself. Cuckooing is therefore a product of the current drug supply and policy environments, just as future drug places will be of theirs. As discussed in this book, historical references to certain other drug places may also linger, both consciously and unconsciously, in the minds of people responding to cuckooing and influence their interpretations of these situations. The 'ghostly' presence of this history (Fiddler et al. 2024), especially regarding 'crack houses', and its influence on the present might even mean it is worth considering the 'past' as a feature of the cuckooing risk environment.

Away from drug spaces, the trap of chronocentrism in the analysis of cuckooing can also be avoided by recognising the depth of criminological insight that has been generated by work that has foregrounded the concept of 'home'. There is, of course, a long tradition of criminological research that has focused on domestic violence, with the home recognised as a site of gendered victimisation (Wykes and Welsh 2008). The relationship between certain types of housing, the housing market and social harm has been the focus of zemiologists (Tombs 2020). The vital role that stable housing can play in desistance from offending and drug use has been well documented (e.g. Low et al. 2023). More broadly, Davies and Rowe (2020) have proposed making the field more coherent through the notion of a 'criminology of the domestic'. All of this work has relevance to cuckooing. At various times throughout this book I have drawn on ideas associated with this body of literature to inform the notion of the cuckooing risk environment. But there is more to be done here and more to be gained by recognising the potential contribution this literature can make. Rather than bracketing off cuckooing as something 'new', separate and distinct and restricting discussions to limited academic reference points specific to the topic, it is important that it is analysed by drawing on a diverse set of concepts and frameworks. This is not only valuable for intellectual enrichment but can also be used to learn lessons and help think more deeply about practical responses. This book's risk environment orientation is my attempt at such an approach. Hopefully other endeavours will follow.

Thinking seriously about the reality of cuckooing

When setting out the aims of this book in the opening chapter I evoked some of the language and analytic framing associated with the perspective of 'left realism' (Matthews 2014). This included the importance of taking cuckooing 'seriously' and a commitment to engaging with its 'reality' – as messy and complex as it may be. As an organising conceptual framework, the risk environment approach has been useful in trying to achieve this. Other approaches with different ontological assumptions would interpret and engage with the concept of cuckooing differently, producing alternative ways of conceiving this drug market problem (see Stevens 2020). Through a Foucauldian lens, for example, the 'problem' of cuckooing might be viewed as a governmental technology that further facilitates the control of certain drug-using populations, with their construction as 'vulnerable individuals' rendering them suitably governable subjects. With the responses to cuckooing similarly interpreted as a further form of surveillance and regime of neoliberal discipline into their private home lives, this might explain why the concept has been so readily adopted by many organisations and institutions. I am not completely averse to this type of theoretical outlook. My previous work has taken a critical stance on the responses to cuckooing (Spicer 2021b), and there have been several analytic threads pertaining to the concept of power raised in the chapters of this book. Such theoretically orientated analyses, if undertaken, could provide some useful insights and ways of thinking about the topic. But there is a risk that such an outlook on cuckooing might offer more dead ends than open avenues in both its analytic capacity and practical implication.

Instead, the risk environment approach adopted in this book has sought to provide a theoretically informed analysis of suitable depth, while keeping in mind the importance of considering practical measures that could be taken to reduce cuckooing and its harms. A central component of this approach has been to demonstrate the deeper processes involved in what, on the surface, can appear as causal features of why cuckooing occurs. Being affected by cuckooing is not simply a result of experiencing poverty, living in poor-quality housing or being drug-dependent. Nor is it simply about there not being harsh enough sentences dished out to those doing the exploiting or enough awareness among practitioners or the public at large about it. There are kernels of truth embedded in all of these. But suggesting that any of them offer sufficient explanations in and of themselves provides a superficial account of cuckooing causation that falls into the trap of what Jock Young referred to as the 'cosmetic fallacy'. This fallacy, he suggests,

> conceives of crime as a superficial problem of society, skin deep, which can be dealt with using the appropriate ointment, rather than as any chronic ailment of society as a whole. It engenders a cosmetic criminology which views crime as a blemish which suitable treatment can remove from a body, which is, itself, otherwise healthy and in little need of reconstruction.
> (Young 1999, p. 130)

One of the reasons 'cosmetic' accounts are attractive is that they suggest that the problem of cuckooing can be solved through simple solutions. As stressed throughout this book, however, the reality of cuckooing is far more complex. A deeper interrogation into what happens in these cases and why is required.

A theoretical tenet running throughout the book conducive to a suitably deep analysis of the reality of cuckooing has been Giddens's (1984) notion of structuration. Understanding cuckooing as a process of structuration recognises the centrality of social structure in producing this drug market-related harm. Simultaneously, it recognises the agency of those affected, where their (constrained) actions involve drawing on the (limited) resources available to them. Often the consequences of these actions are the reproduction of these social structures and their structural position. Various examples of how this plays out in relation to those affected by cuckooing are provided in the previous chapters of this book. The physical environment chapter, for example, showed how someone's negative evaluation of their housing situation might lead to them being less concerned about having other people enter and use it. Yet the outcomes of this 'open door' could be a further deterioration of their home's condition, the experience of being victimised within it and perhaps losing it all together. Similarly, the economic environment chapter discussed how allowing dealers access to a home might pose as attractive to someone excluded from legitimate employment and wanting to avoid the challenges and consequences of illegitimate acquisitive activities. However, the result of this could be further economic marginalisation and exposure to harsh drug market experiences.

What these and the various other examples of structuration demonstrate is that experiences of poverty, poor housing and other structural disadvantages are not simply deterministic reasons why people become affected by cuckooing. Instead, they are important, dynamic features of these people's environment, which are shaped and (re)produced by how they interact with them. Serving as inspiration for this analysis, Alex Stevens' (2011) concept of subterranean structuration proposes a more sophisticated and compelling explanation than simplistic accounts of the drug-crime link. Focused on cuckooing, this book's similar theoretical approach proposes a deeper explanation of why and how this exploitative drug market-related practice occurs. Social structures are central in producing cuckooing and people's vulnerability to being affected. To create an enabling environment for reducing cuckooing and its harms, these structures must be addressed. But the role of human action in the process of cuckooing must also be recognised (Moyle 2019). Rather than ignoring it or falling into forms of victim-blaming when it is identified (Spicer 2021c), an account that acknowledges the presence of agency arguably brings us closer to the 'reality' of cuckooing and, in turn, provides a better way of thinking 'seriously' about it.

Drug market harms and enabling environments

In terms of the contribution of this book, at one level, proposing and developing the notion of a 'cuckooing risk environment' represents a way of generating deeper understandings of cuckooing. Inter alia, this includes producing insights into how this exploitative practice is socially produced, the various processes affected people experience and the (un)intended consequences of the responses enacted against it. On a second level, applying cuckooing to this framework represents a way of contributing to the further development of the risk environment concept itself. As outlined in the introductory chapter, using this public health-oriented approach to analyse the criminological problem of cuckooing is not necessarily the obvious choice. Yet its capacity to consider the various features of the economic, physical, policy and social environments, as well as how these different environments interact at different levels, provides a valuable way of attempting to understand how and why this drug market-related harm occurs. As a discipline that continues to wrestle with the question of individual choice and structural pressure, while often striving for practical orientation based on its findings, criminology could perhaps benefit from incorporating this framework into its analytic toolbox more generally.

Regarding the analytic appropriateness of bringing together this drug market-related harm to the notion of the risk environment, as opposed to this framework's more traditional focus on harms relating to drug use, it is worth reflecting on Fitzgerald's (2009, p. 261) assertion that

> [d]rug dealing poses a particular problem for risk environments as dealing and drug dealers are often thought to be out of the scope of harm reduction interventions. However, local level drug dealing can be an important feature of local economies in marginalised communities, and the sharp distinctions between users and dealers may not always hold.

In the context of cuckooing, the complex roles undertaken by members of marginalised communities in their local drug markets are similarly apparent. Understood as a drug market-related harm, cuckooing involves actors who do not always fit neatly into categories of 'dealer' and 'user', as well as those who problematise broader criminological categories of 'offender' and 'victim'. Incorporating the roles of these different actors into the wider environment that they engage with and shape, while also recognising the capacity for those professionals who respond to cuckooing to (re)produce this environment, makes it possible to conceive of a 'cuckooing risk environment'. From this, it is possible to consider what an 'enabling environment' that would support reducing cuckooing and its harms might look like.

Demonstrating this, as set out in Chapter 4, in the domain of drug policy there are identifiable features of this policy environment that currently appear to produce structural vulnerability to cuckooing. Simultaneously, there are reasons to believe that alternative drug policies could enable reductions in the harms of cuckooing. Similar to arguments regarding 'systemic' violence (Goldstein 1985), the illicit nature of the drug market appears to be an important driver of cuckooing. It pushes various drug market actors together and sets the 'virtually anarchic' (Jacques and Allen 2015) context for their interactions. By viewing drug prohibition as the engine that drives many of the harms associated with the illicit drug market, the proposal of legally regulating the market represents a way of mitigating cuckooing. The other broad drug policy proposal of 'decriminalisation' has typically been orientated far more around drug 'use' rather than drug markets. Indeed, a critique levelled at this policy is its inability to intervene in how illicit drugs are bought and sold. While this critique holds some weight, the analysis in this book suggests that the capacity of decriminalisation in reducing drug market-related harms should not be dismissed. In various ways, criminalising drug possession can create a barrier for effectively engaging with, responding to and safeguarding people affected by cuckooing. The consequences of arrest may even exacerbate the harms of cuckooing and amplify the vulnerability of already vulnerable people (see also Moyle 2019). Ceasing to criminalise people for drug possession could allow for better relationships between them, the police and other agencies, while reducing the contradictions of establishing victim status that currently exist. Some of the experiences and approaches of outreach workers point towards such benefits when pursuing a more harm reduction-orientated approach. Of course, this could also help to reduce their wider structurally marginalised position.

This is not just to suggest that either of these broad drug policy proposals is straightforward in nature or easy to introduce. All drug policy questions are 'genuinely hard' (MacCoun and Reuter 2011). Involving sets of social actors who deploy social power through moral preferences (Stevens 2024), the policymaking process itself is also complex. But it is worth remembering that these are still policy choices. Decisions can be made to do things differently (Ritter 2022). This is not to suggest that these or indeed any other drug policy reforms represent a magic bullet. Introduced by themselves they do not represent panaceas, as tempting as it may be to present them as such (see Spicer 2021a; Young 1999). Instead, they are just one part of the broader cuckooing risk environment. Other types of environments, including various policy types, interact with drug policy, as well as with each other. All of this combines to produce barriers for reducing cuckooing and its harms, while also representing opportunities for making changes and introducing beneficial interventions.

In one sense, then, as an exploitative drug market practice that can severely affect the lives of many people who use drugs, cuckooing should be added to the list of harms that better drug policies could help to reduce. At the same time, the analysis of this book suggests the importance of avoiding myopic thinking. A risk environment approach recognises the potential benefits of 'non-drug' interventions that have the capacity to reduce drug-related harms (Rhodes 2002). As Alex Stevens (2011) has demonstrated, some of the best ways to reduce drug harms are through effective social policy, with reducing inequality perhaps highest on this list. Throughout the various chapters of this book that focus on different types of environments, numerous examples of factors that align with potential 'polythetic' and 'monothetic' interventions (Rhodes 2002) have been identified. It is not my intention to simply list them here. Instead, for the purposes of this concluding discussion, addressing social exclusion and the dynamics associated with inequality can be identified as a broad ambition that encompasses many of these features and has the capacity to ameliorate how cuckooing is socially produced. While cuckooing involves interpersonal exploitation, this regularly sits on top of and interplays with people's experiences of social exclusion and structural violence. Understanding the relationship between the two and breaking this link should arguably be the central overarching concern of a cuckooing-enabling environment.

Across all the different types and levels of environments analysed in this book are features related to this that a cuckooing-enabling environment must address. Economic marginalisation, poor housing and counterproductive responses represent some of the key macro-level drivers of structural vulnerability. At the micro levels, the nature of the interactions within vulnerable communities, the cultural and practical challenges of multi-agency work, and specific features of the physical environment are other examples of how cuckooing can be produced. It is important to understand how these different levels of the cuckooing risk environment interact (Moore and Dietze 2005; Rhodes 2009). The analysis presented in previous chapters has highlighted this interaction, with the process of structuration often being the basis for theoretical explanation. It has also stressed the limitations of responses to cuckooing that overly focus on individual behaviour change or fail to adequately grasp its complex reality. Instead, it is the shuttling back and forth between the macro and micro features of the cuckooing risk environment, combined with the interaction between experiencing the exploitation of cuckooing and the structural exclusion from society that provides a better way of understanding and formulating responses to cuckooing.

This is not to say that certain interventions focused on the level of the individual and promoting behaviour change may not have some benefit. During my time working in this area, I have regularly come across stated desires and embryonic attempts by the police and others to use tools such as risk assessments with those considered at risk to cuckooing. There may well be some value in such tools. But they must be designed and implemented with the insights of the cuckooing risk environment in mind. Asking many of those affected by cuckooing to engage and be honest with police officers and other professionals is not a straightforward task. These responders may have represented a threat to their well-being in the past, played a role in criminalising them or exacerbated their social exclusion throughout their lives (Harding 2020). On the flip side, asking those deemed at risk of cuckooing simply not to engage with dealers or allow anyone into their homes is unlikely to be a sustainable or realistic prospect (Macdonald et al. 2022). While labels such as 'vulnerable' can sometimes rob them of agency, those affected by cuckooing remain social actors. For such monothetic interventions to be effective, they must consider the environmental features of these people's lives and be attuned to their reality. It is by doing so that they have the best chance of beneficially intervening successfully.

Conclusion

From the perspective of an outsider looking in, cuckooing can take on a seductively simplistic appearance, corresponding with simplistic explanatory narratives. These narratives include the 'evil' drug dealer duping the vulnerable user of drugs, the naive local resident opening their door to the dangerous outsider and the 'problem tenant' bringing further troubles to their neighbourhood. At best these tell only a partial story. In reality, cuckooing is regularly the outcome of a range of complex social processes. While it represents a significant drug market-related 'problem' in its own right, people can become affected by pursuing what appear to be solutions to a host of other problems they face in their lives. It is only through understanding these personal problems, their structural origins and how this relates to the process of becoming cuckooed that the problem of cuckooing can be adequately addressed.

The notion of the 'cuckooing risk environment' proposed and developed in this book represents a way of being able to achieve this. It can help reorientate understanding, with its various identifiable features helping to appreciate how it is socially produced. With the environment serving as the unit of analysis, rather than the individuals involved, an agenda for reducing the harms of cuckooing can be developed. Existing barriers can be identified and removed, while suitable interventions that are suitably nuanced can be proposed. Cuckooing is messy and complex. It will remain a difficult problem to solve. But much of the current way it is understood and responded to does not adequately acknowledge or help to unravel this complexity. The notion of the 'cuckooing risk environment' represents an alternative pathway, where this complexity can be suitably acknowledged and the harms of this exploitative practice effectively reduced.

References

Berridge, V. (1978) Victorian opium eating: Responses to opiate use in nineteenth-century England. *Victorian Studies*. 21 (4), pp. 437–461.

Bourgois, P. (1998) Just another night in a shooting gallery. *Theory, Culture & Society*. 15 (2), pp. 37–66.

Davies, P. and Rowe, M. (2020) Towards a criminology of the domestic. *The Howard Journal of Crime and Justice*. 59 (2), pp. 143–157.

Fiddler, M., Linnemann, T. and Kindynis, T. (2024) Ghost criminology: A framework for the discipline's spectral turn. *The British Journal of Criminology*. 64 (1), pp. 1–16.

Fitzgerald, J. L. (2009) Mapping the experience of drug dealing risk environments: An ethnographic case study. *International Journal of Drug Policy*. 20 (3), pp. 261–269.

Giddens, A. (1984) *The Constitution of Society*. Cambridge: Polity.

Goldstein, P. (1985) The drugs/violence nexus: A tripartite conceptual framework. *Journal of Drug Issues*. 15 (4), pp. 493–506.

Harding, S. (2020) *County Lines: Exploitation and Drug Dealing among Urban Street Gangs*. Bristol: Policy Press.

Ingham, J., Purvis, M. and Clarke, D. B. (1999) Hearing places, making spaces: Sonorous geographies, ephemeral rhythms, and the Blackburn warehouse parties. *Environment and Planning D: Society and Space*. 17 (3), pp. 283–305.

Jacques, S. and Allen, A. (2015) Drug market violence: Virtual anarchy, police pressure, predation, and retaliation. *Criminal Justice Review*. 40 (1), pp. 87–99.

Low, G., Lindsay Latimer, C. and Mills, A. (2023) Stable housing, 'home' and desistance: Views from Aotearoa New Zealand. *Criminology & Criminal Justice*. DOI: https://doi.org/10.1177/17488958231210990

MacCoun, R. J. and Reuter, P. (2011) Assessing drug prohibition and its alternatives: A guide for agnostics. *Annual Review of Law and Social Science*. 7 (1), pp. 61–78.

Macdonald, S. J., Donovan, C., Clayton, J. and Husband, M. (2022) Becoming cuckooed: Conceptualising the relationship between disability, home takeovers and criminal exploitation. *Disability & Society*. DOI: https://doi.org/10.1080/09687599.2022.2071680

Matthews, R. (2014) *Realist Criminology*. London: Springer.

Moore, D. and Dietze, P. (2005) Enabling environments and the reduction of drug-related harm: Re-framing Australian policy and practice. *Drug and Alcohol Review*. 24 (3), pp. 275–284.

Moyle, L. (2019) Situating vulnerability and exploitation in street-level drug markets: Cuckooing, commuting, and the 'county lines' drug supply model. *Journal of Drug Issues*. 49 (4), pp. 739–755.

Parkin, S. and Coomber, R. (2009) Informal 'sorter' houses: A qualitative insight of the 'shooting gallery' phenomenon in a UK setting. *Health & Place*. 15 (4), pp. 981–989.

Reinarman, C. and Levine, H. G. (2004) Crack in the rearview mirror: Deconstructing drug war mythology. *Social Justice*. 31 (1/2), pp. 182–199.

Rhodes, T. (2002) The 'risk environment': A framework for understanding and reducing drug-related harm. *International Journal of Drug Policy*. 13 (2), pp. 85–94.

Rhodes, T. (2009) Risk environments and drug harms: A social science for harm reduction approach. *International Journal of Drug Policy*. 20 (3), pp. 193–201.

Ritter, A. (2022) *Drug Policy*. London: Routledge.

Rock, P. (2005) Chronocentrism and British criminology. *The British Journal of Sociology*. 56 (3), pp. 473–491.

Spicer, J. (2021a) Between gang talk and prohibition: The transfer of blame for county lines. *International Journal of Drug Policy*. 87 (1), pp. 29–37.

Spicer, J. (2021b) The policing of cuckooing in 'county lines' drug dealing: An ethnographic study of an amplification spiral. *The British Journal of Criminology*. 61 (5), pp. 1390–1406.

Spicer, J. (2021c) *Policing County Lines*. London: Palgrave.

Stevens, A. (2011) *Drugs, Crime and Public Health*. London: Routledge.

Stevens, A. (2020) Critical realism and the 'ontological politics of drug policy'. *International Journal of Drug Policy*. DOI: https://doi.org/10.1016/j.drugpo.2020.102723

Stevens, A. (2024) *Drug Policy Constellations: The Role of Power and Morality in the Making of Drug Policy in the UK*. Bristol: Policy Press.

Stitt, M. E. and Auyero, J. (2018) Drug market violence comes home: Three sequential pathways. *Social Forces*. 97 (2), pp. 823–840.

Tombs, S. (2020) Home as a site of state-corporate violence: Grenfell Tower, aetiologies and aftermaths. *The Howard Journal of Crime and Justice*. 59 (2), pp. 120–142.

Wykes, M. and Welsh, K. (2008) *Violence, Gender and Justice*. London: Sage.

Young, J. (1999) *The Exclusive Society*. London: Sage.

Index

For Product Safety Concerns and Information please contact our EU representative GPSR@taylorandfrancis.com
Taylor & Francis Verlag GmbH, Kaufingerstraße 24, 80331 München, Germany

www.ingramcontent.com/pod-product-compliance
Lightning Source LLC
Chambersburg PA
CBHW071054280326
41928CB00050B/2512